Agility Training
for you and your dog

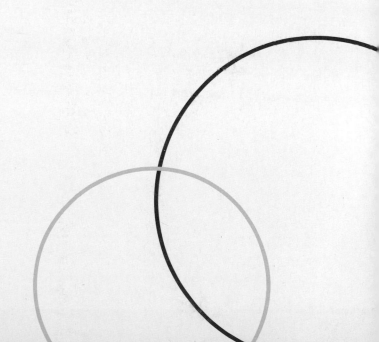

Agility Training
for you and your dog

From Backyard Fun to High-Performance Training

ALI CANOVA and JOE CANOVA with DIANE GOODSPEED

| PHOTOGRAPHS by BRUCE CURTIS |

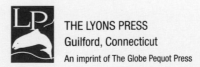

THE LYONS PRESS
Guilford, Connecticut
An imprint of The Globe Pequot Press

It is our dogs who make all the training fun and who teach us about agility and life on a daily basis. They truly are our family and best friends. We dedicate this book to those who have taught us the most: *Argos, Catcher,* and *Wish.*

The Lyons Press is an imprint of The Globe Pequot Press

Designed by Sheryl Kober

Library of Congress Cataloging-in-Publication Data is available on file.

ISBN 978-1-59921-248-7

Printed in China

10 9 8 7 6 5 4 3 2 1

Contents

Acknowledgments

We want to thank Linda Mecklenberg for her insights into jump training and want to thank all of our dedicated Mountain Freaks students, with whom we learn so much and we have such a great time.

Introduction

Through competition classes, private lessons, and intensive topic-oriented seminars, Mountain Freaks Agility in Port Murray, New Jersey, is home to some of the top agility teams in the northeast. Located atop thirteen beautiful acres in rural northwestern New Jersey, the mission of Mountain Freaks Agility is to be a place where people who are serious about the sport of dog agility can gather, train, and grow together. The common bond is that we all love our dogs and we love agility. Building on this bond, owners and directors of Mountain Freaks Agility Ali Canova and Joe Canova have developed and perfected a process for training successful dog agility teams.

In this book Ali and Joe explain their foundation training for successful agility dogs. Both have a long history in competitive agility and have been able to combine their experience and knowledge into a solid, successful program that works for all breeds of dogs and all types of handlers.

About the Trainers

An active, competitor in dog sports since 1993, Ali Canova has trained a wide variety of breeds including English springer spaniels, papillons, golden retrievers, and Border collies. With her Border collies, Ali has become one of America's top agility competitors. Ali's dogs hold multiple championship titles, have been in the United States Dog Agility Association (USDAA) Nationally Ranked Top Ten charts, and have competed in the national finals of USDAA and American Kennel Club (AKC) agility competitions for the last five years. In 2004 Ali and her dog, Wish, became one of the top performing AKC agility teams and were selected as an alternate for the FCI World Championship Team that was sent by the AKC to Italy. In 2005 and 2006, Ali and her Border collie, Catcher, won the Eastern Regional of the Purina Incredible Dog Challenge, and her dogs completed multiple AKC agility

Wish and Ali define intensity on an agility course. (Photo courtesy of Joe Canova)

championships that year. In 2005 and 2006 she was also in the finals at the USDAA National Championships. The team's consistency was showcased at the AKC Agility Championships in January 2006, where Ali was the only handler to qualify two dogs to the final round. Ali and her dogs dominate their height divisions at both AKC and USDAA events, and her dogs are recognized as some of the most consistent performers in competitions, regardless of the venue or level.

Joe Canova has been involved in the sport of dog agility since 1996 and is also a national-level competitor. Joe has had multiple dogs in the national finals of both the AKC and USDAA championships and has qualified for and competed at the AKC World Team Tryouts for several years with his Border collie, Argos, who is an AKC and USDAA agility champion. As codirector and instructor at Mountain Freaks, Joe has helped dozens of handlers become top competitors. He also runs weave, jump, and competition handling seminars throughout the year. In addition, Joe is a professional photographer and has traveled with the USA Agility World Team as official photographer, covering agility world championships in Italy, Portugal, and Germany. He has also photographed national championships for the *AKC Gazette* and *Clean Run Magazine*. Joe is a chiropractic physician and has also done animal chiropractic work.

CHAPTER 1

The Sport of Agility

Pairs ice-skating requires balance, flow, precision, speed, and trust between partners. The accuracy and pace of a successful performance are inspiring. Each partner relies on and communicates with the other to achieve perfection. Although the team members have different abilities and skills, each blends his or her performance into the other's to form a cohesive, balanced partnership. Neither member can perform alone.

Like pairs skating, agility is a team sport. A flowing, accurate performance is based on precision teamwork. Canine and human partners work together—interpreting and functioning in unison—to successfully navigate a demanding obstacle course. Using a shared language, often unique to each team, human and canine blend their efforts and skills to perform together, pushing for speed and accuracy on every curve, turn, and straight line. Agility showcases each species' ability to communicate and function together.

Racing all out to the finish line.

Agility dogs are agile and fast. (Photo courtesy of Joe Canova)

Each team member has a different task. Racing against the clock, handlers must direct their dogs to jump, climb ramps, navigate through tunnels, traverse a seesaw, and weave through a line of poles in a configuration designed to challenge. It is the handler's job to direct the dog to the correct obstacle and ensure a safe execution. The dog is responsible for the actual obstacle performance. The precision beneath the team's accuracy and dynamic flow is based on the *relationship* between the dog and handler. An outstanding course run has an inherent rhythm and balance and elicits applause from spectators, whether the team is a beginner or seasoned competitor. It is this display of the human-dog bond that has made agility the fastest-growing dog sport in America for almost a decade.

Agility made its debut in 1978 as a demonstration at the United Kingdom's Crufts Dog Show. Conceived by John Varley, the event was intended to entertain the crowd during the spare time in the main arena between the end of the obedience championships and the commencement of the group breed judging. What evolved was the brainchild of Peter Meanwell. He used an equestrian show jumping format

Agility offers a multitude of competition levels and events.

to showcase the canine's strength, speed, and agility over a variety of equipment, including the seesaw, weave poles, pause table, and several jumps. Using a simple course flow, Meanwell wanted an event that was safe and fun for the dogs while providing spectator appeal. With two teams of four dogs, he succeeded dramatically. The crowd loved it, and the dogs loved it. By 1979 several British dog training clubs were training agility dogs and the first Agility Stakes competition was held at the International Horse Show in London that December. In 1980 the British Kennel Club became the first organization to recognize agility as an official sport with a sanctioned set of rules.

Dog agility grew quickly into a unique sport that spread around the globe. In 1985 Kenneth Tatsch, having seen agility in England, began putting on agility exhibitions in Texas, and within a year he founded the USDAA. The first national championship tournament series in North America—the Grand Prix of Dog Agility—was held in 1988 at the Astro World Series of Dog Shows in Houston, Texas. In 1990 USDAA began offering agility titles, and a half dozen existing and new dog organizations quickly followed with their own sanctioned agility events. In

1993 the North American Dog Agility Council (NADAC) was formed, and in 1994 the AKC held its first agility trial in Texas. Within a few years, agility competitions were being held in all fifty states, making agility the fastest-growing dog sport in America. In the first year of AKC agility, there were 23 trials with about 2,000 entries. By 2003 there were 1,379 trials. By 2007 the number of AKC trials in the United States exceeded 2,000.

As the sport grew in popularity in the United States, it began to homogenize. The basic rules and requirements to compete stabilized across venues, and the equipment began to become standardized. Although the different organizations that sponsor agility competitions continue to be unique and have slightly different equipment requirements, most now use the same basic pieces of equipment.

Today's agility consists of four types of equipment: jumps, tunnels, weave poles, and contacts, which are the dog walk, seesaw, pause table, and A-frame. The dog walk is a series of three ten-inch- or twelve-inch-wide planks connected into a raised walk. The length and height of the dog walk can vary. The seesaw is a teeter-totter. The dog walks up to the tip point and rides the plank down. A pause table is a flat, raised table on which the dog must pause for several seconds. The A-frame is a set of four-foot-wide boards connected and raised into an A shape. The height of the A-frame varies by organization. Many of these pieces of equipment are now incorporated at lower heights in many dog parks and in dog play areas. All the basic training for each piece of equipment is covered in this book—for all levels of enjoyment.

Whether you are exploring dog agility for fun or for competition, the advantages are numerous and the benefits do not depend on the level or intensity of your training. First and foremost, agility is super fun for dogs and great exercise for you both. Racing through tunnels, leaping jumps, and charging up an A-frame offer dogs high-intensity exercise. It is recess—supersized! Many of the working breeds thrive on this level of activity. Agility also builds confidence. Dogs learn assurance and self-reliance as they figure out how to cross the dog walk, navigate through a curved tunnel, or bounce through a series of jumps. Through agility training, dogs learn to believe in their own abilities. In addition, agility offers dog owners a chance to bond with their dogs. It requires that you function as a team and, as such, your relationship with your dog evolves. These new dimensions in the canine-human relationship are what make agility so enjoyable.

At Mountain Freaks Agility, Ali and Joe focus primarily on this relationship between dog and handler. Their methods and techniques build and then reinforce this bond between teammates from equipment introduction to sequence training. Whether you are training for pure fun or for competition, the agility training described in this book will ensure an improved relationship with your canine pal. Using the training methodology of Mountain Freaks, you can enjoy agility with your dog in your backyard, at the dog park, in a group class at your local dog club, or at a national competition.

CHAPTER 2

The Team

In a sport where precision and speed are equally important, the team must be balanced and controlled. Both dog and handler must learn a wide range of skills to achieve trust and stability so that each member can rely on and work off the other. Agility begins with the equipment performance, which is the dog's job. It then changes slightly as pieces of equipment are connected in short sequences. For example, you may ask your dog to do a jump, then go to the seesaw, and then onto the pause table. At the short sequence level, the dog and handler must begin to function as a team. Once the team is flowing together, the dog and handler can work on long sequences and then on a full course, which consists of fourteen to twenty obstacles set in a prearranged order. Communication between dog and handler grows in importance at every level. And yet, every team is unique. Every pair develops its own nuances and communication pathways. Ultimately, teamwork is what makes agility addictive fun for both members of the team.

Beyond the fun factor and the incredible thrills found in competition, there are multiple advantages to agility training for both teammates.

- TEAMWORK
  The trust and communication built into your relationship as you train are priceless. Relying on and communicating with each other, you, the human member, evolve from trainer to partner. This conversion is exhilarating. It strengthens the bond between you and your dog and turns mere coopera-tion into a true connection. And this connection is permanent and exists off the agility course as well. As your working partner, your agility dog bonds to you in a deep, enduring friendship.

A front cross alerts the dog to a change in direction. (Photo courtesy of Joe Canova)

- CONFIDENCE

  A common phenomenon in agility is the handler who takes a shy, nervous dog to class for fun and ends up competing for years with a confident, athletic dog. Worried, nervous dogs gain assurance during agility training. They become confident in their own abilities and become joyful playmates. The transition of a shy, skittish dog into a rambunctious, playful creature is a true joy to watch.

- PLAYTIME

  Put simply, agility is recess with your dog. It is compelling. You do not have to compete to enjoy the sport. As its popularity grows, local clubs and 4-H groups offer more and more fun agility events, and many townships have incorporated agility equipment into their dog parks. An agility class once a week may be enough for you to enjoy this sport with your dog. Alternately, you (or your dog) may get so enthused that you end up purchasing a full set of equipment for your backyard!

Agility is a wonderful sport for every dog breed. (Photo courtesy of Joe Canova)

- EXERCISE

  Agility is physically demanding. An hour class can provide plenty of exercise for your dog and you. As you progress into short sequences and full course work, the phrase—"run for fun" can take on a whole new meaning!

- VARIETY

  With multiple agility registries offering a variety of classes and levels of competition, agility has something for every dog, every handler, and every team. There are classes that emphasize jumping ability, classes for dog's that love tunnels, classes that depend on strategy, and classes that reward consistency. Many of the largest agility organizations in the United States are described in chapter 12.

Whether you use agility for playtime, exercise, or competition, the strength of your team begins with its members: dog and handler.

The Dog

All dogs are not created equal. Although all dogs are a single species, their body size, color, inherent abilities, and temperaments vary enormously. For hundreds of years specific traits were bred into specific breeds. Many of these selected traits drive behavior and are *part of the dog*. For instance, it is very difficult to remove the herding instinct from a Border collie or the hunting instincts from a Welsh springer spaniel. In any breed, and even within the same litter, some dogs display more inherent instincts than others, but the critical factor is to recognize what your dog's natural instincts tell him to do. If your dog's core (or soul) has a hunting dog lurking there, he is going to hunt. If your dog's core breeding tells him to herd, he will herd whatever is around—you, a duck, or the neighbor's cat. If your dog has basically been bred to be a house pet, you may actually have to encourage him to walk on grass and may need to beg to get him over mud.

None of this should unduly impact your desire to train your dog in agility. It just means every dog needs to be evaluated, trained, and handled a little differently. Agility is a wonderful sport for every dog breed from Yorkshire terrier to Bernese mountain dog.

The type of dog may pose certain challenges in training and handling, but no dogs are excluded. Thus, agility is frequently referred to as a "sport for all dogs."

AGE CONSIDERATIONS

What ages are appropriate for agility? There are guidelines but no real rules. Puppies under six months of age are generally not coordinated enough to begin agility training. Furthermore, they should not be in public places until they have all their vaccinations and are protected from disease. Run your puppy around the yard or a quiet park and get him used to wearing a collar, walking on a leash, playing with toys, and walking with you. Once your puppy is between three and six months of age, attend a puppy kindergarten or beginner obedience class, which often incorporates tunnels and tippy boards during puppy

Puppy play with the tunnel can begin at an early age.

playtime. Look for a class that emphasizes handler-dog interactions and that teaches simple obedience using positive reinforcement.

Once they are seven or eight months old, most puppies can begin agility training. Puppies love tunnels and enjoy playing on equipment set on the floor or at puppy height and love to chase around their human buddy. The limiting issues are physical development and mental control. During the first year, bones are growing, joints are forming, and the dog's personality is still developing. Excessive wear and tear—on the body or mind—during this growth time can lead to serious problems in an adult dog. However, these youngsters have natural enthusiasm and energy. Agility training channels this energy and helps develop a strong bond between dog and handler. So to avoid injury and stress, keep training sessions short, jump heights low, and the exercises fun.

Older dogs should be evaluated on their fitness level, overall health, and ability to be controlled rather than their age.

FITNESS EVALUATION

Dogs are no different than people. They live healthier, happier lives with good nutrition, daily exercise, and a few common sense precautions, such as vaccines and preventive medical care. You need to consider your dog's physical condition very carefully before adding new activities to his life. There are a lot of couch potatoes out there in the canine world. The quality of your dog's experience and the level of fun for you as his partner in agility are directly proportional to the care and preparation provided before you start.

Today one in every three dogs in the United States is overweight. The risks of being overweight are the same whether you have two legs or four and include diabetes, heart disease, joint problems, cancer, and a shortened life span. The physical demands of agility can be downright dangerous for an overweight dog. So how exactly do you determine if your dog is overweight? There are three simple tests that will get you started on an answer. For long-haired or double-coated dogs, check the follow when the dog is soaking wet.

With no sweat glands and only panting available to disperse body heat, dogs are much more susceptible to heatstroke than we are. Your dog cannot remove his coat and cannot always sense when to rest. Unusually rapid panting, a bright red tongue, and/or staggering are signs of heat exhaustion. If any of these signs occur, you need to cool your dog down immediately. Put cool water or cool cloths under the legs, on the feet, and on the tummy. Do not put cool water on the dog's back. Keep the dog quiet and in a cool spot. Offer plenty of water. If ice cubes or ice pops are available, let your dog chew the ice in small amounts. Resume activity slowly. Common sense, good conditioning, and plenty of water can minimize the risk of heatstroke.

Ribs

With your dog standing, press gently on the skin over the ribs. You should be able to feel the ribs without pressing. If you have to press hard to feel rib bones, then your dog is probably overweight.

Waist

Stand over or just slightly behind your dog while he is standing and look for a waistline. A slight indentation or tuck should be visible just behind the ribs and before the hips. This is your dog's waist. If the waist is not clearly visible, your dog is probably overweight.

Abdomen

While your dog is standing, look at him from the side. You should see a distinct tuck or curve between the rib cage and hind legs. If the abdomen is not visible, your dog is probably overweight.

Agility is physically intense for both dog and handler. If you are not sure about your dog's fitness level, or you know for sure your dog needs to get started on an exercise program, take your dog for long walks before you enroll in a class or begin agility training. Walk, walk, and then walk some more. Go around the block several times a day and then increase the distance gradually. You should also acclimate your dog to different temperatures. When you start your dog's fitness program or early agility training, avoid the hotter parts of the day; dogs have a tough time ridding themselves of heat.

HEALTH CHECK

The second step is a visit to your veterinarian. Like humans, dogs should not be started on a diet and exercise program without first making sure that the extra weight is truly from overeating and/or a lack of exercise. If your dog does need to go on a diet, help him to remove the weight gradually. Ask your veterinarian for alternate foods and think carefully about how many snacks, table scraps, and treats your dog gets. This is critical as you begin training more. A few diet changes and a regular exercise program will get your dog started on a healthier lifestyle and into agility training in no time.

Another important health consideration is spaying/neutering your pet. If your dog is not part of a breeding program, spay (female) or neuter (male) your pet. It is healthier for your pet and eliminates potential behavior problems.

CONTROLABILITY

You must also evaluate your dog's behavior. If you have a shy or nervous dog, the noise level and energy in an agility class may frighten him. A low-key obedience, rally, or pet tricks class can give your dog a chance to learn to focus and learn around other dogs, without the stress of navigating agility equipment. Alternately, many of the breeds that excel at agility have a high tolerance for activity, but this tolerance also comes with a high prey drive, which is the basic instinct to chase. All the activity and motion in agility class can be overstimulating. It is not uncommon for dogs to get overexcited and lose their ability to focus on you or their training. For a dog with high prey drive, agility class may be too much excitement. Furthermore, if you have a dog that is not well socialized or shows signs of aggression, agility class can quickly bring out the worst in your dog. With aggressive or high prey drive dogs, we recommend several obedience classes before you start agility classes. You must have control of your dog—in every situation—before you can begin agility.

The Handler

Keeping track of your dog, the sequence of obstacles, and your own path through an agility course is physically and mentally challenging. Furthermore, the intensity of the activity increases proportionally with the speed of the dog. Agility requires you to be both your dog's trainer and his partner. This unique mix makes agility exciting and fun. It also makes it difficult. As a team member, you—the handler—must also evaluate your own interests, skills, and fitness level.

INTEREST LEVEL

Agility provides great exercise and entertainment. It is also a highly competitive, speed sport. For you and your dog, it can be entertainment, competition, or both. Enrolling in a beginner class for fun is common in agility. Most instructors incorporate a multitude of desires and goals in classes. When you enroll in a class, be sure to express your current goals to your instructor.

Whether you are training for fun or competition, the first phase of agility training is to teach the dog the equipment, including tunnels, weave poles, jumps, pause table, and the contact obstacles (dog walk, A-frame, seesaw). Once the dog understands how to approach and execute all the individual pieces of equipment, the human half of the team must learn how to direct the dog through a short sequence of obstacles. Often the handler—after months of agility classes—is basically untrained! This often comes as a surprise to many handlers. Keep in mind that training the dog on the equipment is only the beginning of the process, though there is overlap. As a dog learns a new piece of equipment, it can be inserted into short sequences, which gives the handler a chance to work on timing and communication. Agility training, however, takes several years, and even the most accomplished dogs with experienced handlers often take eighteen to twenty months to advance to full course work. Of course, every step of the process is fun and challenging!

AGE CONSIDERATIONS

Learning to juggle your performance and your dog's takes practice and patience. To this end, the age of the handler is also a consideration. Most youngsters need to be at least eleven or twelve before they begin training an agility dog. If your child has trained a dog in obedience or rally or has a competitive sports background, then he or she may be able to start a little earlier. It is also easier for younger handlers to begin agility if they work an experienced agility dog. This reduces or eliminates the equipment introduction and training phases and allows the child to focus on performance. If you have a novice dog and junior handler team, enroll them in an obedience or rally class first to ensure effective communication and to attain mutual cooperation before they begin agility. Basic obedience training can also provide your child with a better understanding of the principles of dog training, such as consistency, effective rewards, and positive reinforcement. These may or may not be part of a beginner agility class, which focuses on training the dog to perform each obstacle.

PHYSICAL CHALLENGES

Agility is physically demanding. It requires agility from both team members. Before you engage in a high-speed run around an obstacle course on an uneven or wet surface with your dog, consider your own age and joint development (or deterioration). The abrupt starting, stopping, and turning required of an agility handler can cause injury to unwary knees and ankles. In fact injured handlers are more common in agility than injured dogs!

You must follow the same guidelines for yourself as you did for your dog. Before you enroll in a class, evaluate your own fitness level and set your goals accordingly. A handler with physical challenges or limits simply requires a different set of skills, much like a handler with an extremely fast dog or with a tiny dog. Be sure to explain these limits to your instructor so class work and drills can build the skills you will need to proceed with your dog's training.

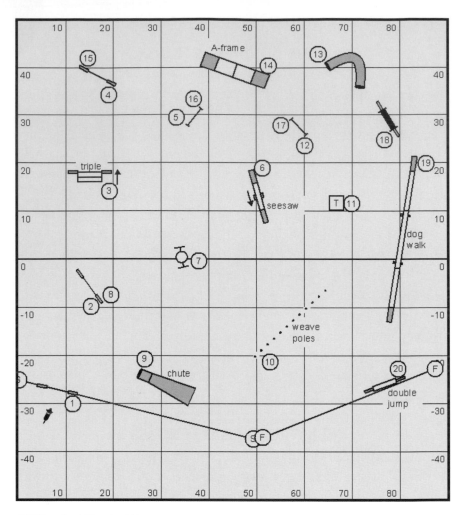

AKC Excellent Standard Course

It is also important for the handler to wear appropriate shoes and clothing. Zip up or remove loose clothing that can catch on agility equipment. Do not try to train or run in dress shoes or sandals. Wear shoes with treads and ankle support. If you are training outdoors on grass or dirt, invest in shoes that have a distinct raised tread, such as cross trainers or turf shoes. These are absolutely necessary for running on damp or extremely dry grass. If you are training indoors on rubber mats or carpet, purchase shoes with a flatter bottom, such as running or tennis shoes, to prevent snagging cleats on edges or loose threads.

Analyzing a course through a crowd can be difficult.

MENTAL CHALLENGES

Mental acuity is also needed for agility training. Remembering the course sequence, your path, the dog's path, and the rules for the class you are running—all while directing your partner at full speed—is not for everyone. Unless you have your dog trained to read numbers, it is your job to direct the dog through each sequence or course. At the highest level of competition, there can be anywhere from eighteen to twenty obstacles with a path that doubles back multiple times over the same obstacle.

In addition to memorizing your dog's path in a short, ten-minute walk-through, you must also know where you need to be at any given point to give those directions. During the walk-through, which is a set time before an agility competition begins when the handlers can review and analyze the course, there may be twenty, forty, or even sixty other people walking the course at the same time. And, of course, agility is the "sport of the unexpected." When running the course you must also learn to adjust and revise your position and location to help your teammate succeed.

If you have trouble remembering sequences or stress quickly in competitive situations, try rally or obedience before advancing into agility. If agility is a passion, go to matches, drop in to different agility classes, and try the games classes, such as NADAC tunnelers [see page 233] or CPE colors [see page 230]. All of these offer different situations in which to practice and play with your dog, before you try more stressful environments or more competitive classes.

CHAPTER 3

Getting Started

The Mountain Freaks methodology is simple and is used for every dog. Though the methodology is the same for different breeds and ages, the actual training may vary, depending on the speed at which the dog learns and the temperament of the dog. The basic tenants are introduce, train, and then proof. Every exercise is introduced gently with an emphasis on consistency and clarity. We introduce each exercise in detail and explain how to fix common problems. The introduction is followed by practice drills. These training exercises expand your dog's understanding of the required behavior. The final piece is proofing. Testing or proofing your dog's knowledge and understanding requires creativity and patience but guarantees the consistent performance needed in a confident, winning team.

Another distinctive component to the Mountain Freaks methodology is the interwoven training methods. For example, the introduction to jumping is used as a warm-up before class or a course run. Groundwork drills are used during short sequence work to clean up lines and clarify body language communication. We use jump chutes, circles, and grids to keep our dogs' jumping accurate while trialing and pushing for speed. Every exercise and drill has multiple purposes and is used throughout the dog's competitive career.

The Freaks Process

These are the fives stages of the Mountain Freaks process:

- OBEDIENCE BASICS
  The dog must be under control and be willing to pay attention to his handler. Basic obedience commands for agility include *Come, Wait, Sit,* and *Down.*

- GROUNDWORK TRAINING
  You must be able to direct your dog between obstacles. Groundwork trains the dog and handler to move together as a team between the various pieces of equipment.

- EQUIPMENT INTRODUCTION
  Every obstacle—jumps, tunnels, seesaw, pause table, A-frame, dog walk, and weaves—must be trained individually.

- SHORT SEQUENCE WORK
  At this level the team negotiates a short series of obstacles. A short sequence usually has three or four obstacles. The types of obstacles used depend on the dog's age and competence on the equipment. Early sequence training can be simply tunnel-to-tunnel, while a more advanced short sequence might be seesaw-tunnel-weaves.

- FULL COURSE WORK
  This is the precompetition level. Agility teams should be able to navigate successfully through a series of fourteen to twenty obstacles once they are ready to attend fun matches or enter a competition.

Every stage is worked in order but every level overlaps and interacts with the previous. In other words, you are never done training obedience basics, groundwork, equipment performance, and short sequence work. One of the main reasons Mountain Freak dogs become top competitors is the interwoven training. For example, groundwork is trained on a solid obedience foundation, incorporated immediately into equipment training, and then reinforced throughout short sequence work. Equipment is introduced with methods and exercises that are used in short sequence work to clarify your dog's performance to ensure consistency and to keep your dog's enthusiasm high.

Young dogs should progress through the early stages of agility training at an easy pace. You must balance their ability to focus with their developing physical abilities. Older dogs can progress at a more rapid pace.

Agility is a fantastic game for dogs and humans. (Photo courtesy of Joe Canova)

Training Equipment Requirements

One of the first questions many beginners ask is, "How much equipment do I need to purchase?" The answer is, "None." You can and should begin agility training at a training facility or public park that provides access to the various pieces of equipment. You do not need to purchase expensive contacts, such as a dog walk seesaw, tunnels, or weaves, to begin agility training. As you progress through the training stages, you can decide what pieces of equipment best support your dog's training. Many, many people train agility without ever owning a piece of agility equipment. Others own a few jumps, weave poles, and, perhaps, a plank on which to train the basics of the dog walk or seesaw.

The equipment you do need for agility training is surprisingly simple.

WATER, BAGS, AND CRATES

Regardless of where you train, always bring along a water bowl and provide your dog with fresh water. Agility is exercise, and your dog is doing a lot of it. Take frequent breaks, especially during warm weather.

Another requirement is pooper-scooper bags. If you are training in a public area, you must carry poop bags and, even more important, you must use them. Potty your dog, before you start training. This may take a few minutes, but the time is well spent. Your instructor may also recommend a portable crate. A crate allows you to give your dog a rest period and/or allows you to focus on instructions, walk a sequence, or practice your own moves—all without worrying about what your pooch is doing while your attention is elsewhere.

Dogs do not need nor derive any benefit from sports drinks such as Gatorade. These drinks contain a balanced mix of water, sugar (carbohydrates), and salts (electrolytes) and are effective for hydrating human athletes. Dogs do not need sugar and salt to hydrate or rejuvenate tired muscles. Offer lots of water and drink the Gatorade yourself.

COLLAR

A simple buckle or quick-snap collar is preferred. Either leather or nylon is fine. Prong, choke, and shock collars are not necessary. These are training tools for specific behavior problems, which need to be worked out *before* you begin agility training. Similarly, harnesses and haltees are not used in agility training. These devices can catch on equipment and impede your dog's motion and visibility. Furthermore, remove swinging tags or keep a separate collar for training. During training, particularly with jump drills, every takeoff and landing can cause tags to bop your dog in the chin and neck.

LEASH

Choose a sturdy four- or six-foot leash. It can be either nylon or leather but not a retractable. Flexible-length leashes are too long and tangle easily with equipment. Select a lightweight leash with a minimum width, which allows you to gather the leash in your hand. Thin slip leads are also acceptable.

TOYS

Purchase a toy that your dog will chase and play tug with. Soft fuzzy toys and rope-like toys work well. If you are training in a group, avoid tennis balls and Frisbees, since you may end up rewarding someone else's dog. Also keep in mind that for agility exercises, the toy is frequently carried in your hand or placed in a pocket. Select a small or medium-size toy, not a six-foot fuzzy snake. Keep your dog's training toys separate from his playtime toys. This keeps his drive and enthusiasm high during training.

Some dogs learn chase and tug easier than others. With a dog that does not play immediately or with enthusiasm, we try a variety of games. First, play with different toys until your dog has a favorite. Many dogs engage quickly if the toy makes a sound, such as a squeak, or has a distinct smell, such as a leather work glove. Second, attach the toy to an eight-foot string and lure your dog into a game of chase. Many dogs, particularly terriers and hounds, engage quickly when the toy is constantly moving. And finally, there are specialty toys that have pouches for food. These fuzzy half-breeds are a good choice for dogs with high food drive but low toy drive. With food-toy hybrids your dog must retrieve the toy and bring it to you. Do not run to the toy and offer a treat. Your dog must bring you the toy.

Also keep in mind that toys are for playing. The game, however, cannot be between the dog and the toy! It must include you. Do not give your dog a toy and let him play with it by himself. Use toys to play with your dog. We never allow a dog to grab his toy and do a "victory lap" around the building. The dog must grab the toy and bring it to you to toss or for a game of tug. If your dog habitually leaves with his toy, put the toy on a string and reel him in. A string lets you control the toy.

You should also attach a verbal command to toy games. When playing tug with your dog, say *Tug!* When tossing the ball, say *Get it!* With a word, you can communicate with your dog. You can tell him which game you are going to play. This can help build drive and keep your dog engaged with you. Your dog is more likely to "share" his toy with you for a game of tug! For toy-driven dogs you also want to use a verbal command that ends the game. Common choices are *Leave it* or *All done.*

TREATS

You will also need treats—lots and lots of treats! Soft treats that your dog can eat easily and quickly are best. Hard treats, such as pieces of dog biscuit, are hard for dogs to eat on the go. Not only does chewing take too long, if your dog has to chew the treat, he will stop. If he does not stop to chew, the treat becomes a choking hazard. Treats that crumble also cause difficulties. It is too easy to drop pieces of food on the floor or in the grass. Food-motivated dogs will stop for every crumb! If you use baked chicken, cut lumps and split them into pieces as you train.

Treats must also be readily accessible. Use treats that can be placed in a pocket or treat pouch or carried by the dozens in your hand. Never carry treats in your mouth. Although this is popular for obedience training, agility is an active, physical sport, which increases the likelihood of you choking on the treat. Furthermore, unlike obedience, you do not want your dog focused on your face. You want your dog focused on your body position and hand.

Also keep in mind the color of the treat versus the surface on which you are training. If you are training on grass, use a light-colored treat. Conversely, if you are training indoors on gray or green mats, use a dark-colored treat. This is important if you are training an exercise that requires you to drop a treat on the ground, such as with initial jump training or for a target drill.

Treat rewards should be bite-size or smaller. Little dogs need little pieces and big dogs need little pieces! Do not offer huge treats just because your dog is big. Think in terms of kibble size. Treats should be bite-size so you can give out lots of them during a training session without filling up your dog's belly. Commercial treats work just as well as thin-sliced hot dogs, chunks of string cheese, or cooked chicken chunks. If you are using hot dogs or string cheese, slice them in circles, which are easy to hold in your hand and dispense quickly.

Treat Recipes

Your dog deserves the best! You know it. And your dog definitely knows it. So why not whip up some homemade treats to show your four-footed pal how much you care? The following recipes contain all natural ingredients. Every recipe has been time-tested by fantastic agility dogs, and every effort has been made to remove those foods that are not healthy for dogs. And, last but not least, all the wholesome ingredients can be found in your typical large grocery store. So head for the kitchen and get cookin'.

Health Tip

The American Society for the Prevention of Cruelty to Animals (ASPCA) lists all of the following as potentially harmful to dogs:

• Chocolate (baker's, semi-sweet, and milk)
• Raisins and grapes
• Salt
• Alcohol
• Coffee
• Onion (including onion powder)
• Garlic (including garlic powder)
• Fatty foods (including bacon grease)

They also list avocados, hops, macadamia nuts, and yeast dough as possibly dangerous to dogs. There are also dogs with wheat allergies. The wheat flour in any of these recipes can be changed to rice or oat bran flour.

Gooey Blobs

From gooey to chewy, these colorless blobs are tasty soft treats. They are very good treats for young dogs since the ingredients are easy on puppy tummies. Gooey blobs do not crumble so bake big (1–2 inches) and break off pieces as you train. It is also an easy recipe to double or triple.

Ingredients
2 jars beef or chicken baby food (2.5-ounce size)
¼ cup dry milk powder
¼ cup wheat germ

Directions
Preheat oven to 350 °F. Combine all ingredients and mix well. Drop by teaspoonfuls onto a well-greased cookie sheet and bake ten to twelve minutes until brown. Refrigerate to keep fresh. Makes about a dozen medium-size cookies.

Beefy Beer Bait

Need a treat to beef up your pup's performance? Or maybe just to jazz up that anxious pooch? Or perhaps to get your hound to focus? Beefy beer bait is your best bet. Simple and easy to make, this stuff will get an enthusiastic response.

Ingredients
1 pound beef (London broil or sirloin steak)
1 cup teriyaki sauce (low-sodium variety)
1 12-ounce bottle dark ale

Directions
Cut steak in strips about 1-inch wide and $1/_5$-inch thick. To facilitate cutting, put meat in the freezer until it is stiff but not frozen. Marinate the beef strips in teriyaki sauce overnight. Sit down, put up your feet, drink the ale, and give some serious thought as to *why* you are feeding your dog sirloin steak! In the morning, preheat oven to 200°F and spread the marinated steak on a tinfoil-covered baking sheet. Bake thirty minutes and then flip. Bake the second side for fifteen to twenty minutes or until dry. Store in the refrigerator in an airtight container. Makes about ten to fifteen strips that are easy to shred into treat-size pieces.

Banana Bites

This variation on the classic Milk-Bone biscuit recipe yields a soft, break-able treat that disappears down canine throats at a phenomenal rate. They are also easy to carry in pockets, without the slimy mess of meat chunks, and make great tossing treats.

Ingredients
½ cup hot water
1 medium-size, ripe banana (mashed)
½ cup powdered milk
1 egg (beaten)
3 cups whole wheat or oat bran flour

Directions
Preheat oven to 250°F. In a large bowl pour hot water over the banana. Stir in powdered milk and egg. Add flour, one cup at a time, until you have a stiff dough. Move dough to a lightly floured surface and roll to ¼-inch thickness. Cut dough into kibble-size squares or use a small cookie cutter. Bake on an ungreased cookie sheet for fifteen to twenty minutes and remove from cookie sheet immediately. Makes about four cups of treats.

CHAPTER 4

Obedience Basics

Basic obedience is the cornerstone of your canine communication skills. Obedience training gives you a "language" with which to communicate with your dog and, hopefully, teaches your dog that you mean what you say. With positive reinforcement training, the use of treats and toys also makes the process fun and relatively simple. Dogs are pack animals. They inherently know that rules exist and are to be followed. The problem is getting the dog to agree that it is *your* rules by which the pack must live. The simplest, shortest path to a well-behaved dog is through a course at the nearest dog training school that offers a beginner obedience class or an attention and handling class.

An obedience course will serve you and your pet well and is relatively inexpensive. A qualified instructor can provide feedback particular to your dog and your training and can tailor the drills to your specific needs. Be sure to let the instructor know what you want from the class. Furthermore, going to dog school provides your dog an opportunity to mingle with his own kind and to learn manners. An eight-week session or two six-week sessions of obedience classes should provide basic training for the commands *With Me, Sit, Down, Stay, Wait,* and *Come.* For experienced owners, much of this training can also be done at home. However you handle his training, your dog needs the following *before* you begin agility.

Name Recognition

Many obedience instructors joke that 50 percent of the dogs that begin class firmly believe their name is "No!" Does your dog *know* his name?

What do you expect him to do when he hears it? Is it a substitute for *Come*? Is it merely a "Hey, you!" Or does it mean "Run for your life!" In obedience and agility training, calling your dog's name should get his attention. It is not a substitute for *Come*. It is not a correction. It should not be negative. Hearing his name, your dog should focus, pay attention, and look at you.

Your dog's name is used to gain his attention prior to issuing a command. It is the "start your engine" command. It does not mean "move forward." Hearing his name should alert your dog to an incoming command or redirection on course. It means "watch me" or "look at me for more information."

> **Training Tip**
>
> The dog's name is also not a release. It does not mean *Move*. Although experienced trainers who worked multiple dogs do use their dogs' names as releases, most trainers keep the dog's name on reserve.

Once your dog is focused, you can issue a command or move onto the next sequence.

On the other hand you do not want to say your dog's name before every obstacle. It is not, "Fido! Jump. Fido! Jump. Fido! Tunnel." If you use your dog's name between obstacles, you are interrupting the flow by asking for his attention before every obstacle. If you say his name, he should look at you. Although these constant check-ins and redirects may be necessary on a difficult agility course, they are not needed in early training, where the obstacle is directly in front of the dog. Using your dog's name when you do not want his attention dilutes its meaning and your dog's response to it. If you say his name without needing and demanding his attention, you will not get it later when you truly need it.

Since your dog's name is used to gain his attention and is used immediately before a command, you also want a short name. If your dog's name has multiple syllables, such as Baccarat, Dandelion, or Maximillion, you need to come up with a short form of your dog's name. On an agility course you do not have time to say "Dandelion! Tunnel!" By the time you get done saying "Dandelion!" your dog will already be off-course skidding happily across the seesaw. Try for a one- or two-syllable, easy-to-say short version of your dog's name. For example, shorten Dandelion to Dani or Maximillion to Max. You also want your dog's name to sound distinctly different from any of your commands. For example if you shorten Baccarat to Bac, then do not use the common *Back* command to teach your dog to turn away from you. Pick something else for *Back,* such as *Flip* or *Turn.*

If possible, when you are choosing your dog's short name, use a word that begins with a hard consonant such as *D, B, G,* or *N,* versus a soft consonant such as *S, F,* or *H.* Your dog, particularly a high-drive dog, may only have time to register one sound while making his decision about where to go. Make the sound count. And you might want to stay away from names that begin with *T.* There are multiple agility obstacles that begin with *T,* including the pause table, tire jump, tunnel, and teeter. If your dog's short name begins with a *T,* then vary the obstacles' names. Use *Park* for table, *Thru* for the tire, or *Seesaw* for teeter. The point is to avoid having multiple commands and your dog's name begin with the same sound.

Work Mode

Focus—the ability to pay attention—is the difference between a pet and a working dog. The working animal understands when he is working. In order to begin agility training, your dog should be capable of paying attention to you. Often referred to by trainers as a "work mode," this is an important skill. If your dog is sniffing the ground or posturing for another dog, he cannot learn from you. Furthermore, you cannot call your dog off every distraction. He must be taught to pay attention. Some dogs, particularly working breeds such as the Border collies, Dobermans, and Labradors, may come packaged with this skill or pick it up immediately. For many breeds, focus is a learned skill. It must be developed during early obedience training and before you begin agility training.

Puppies tend to have very short attention spans, so work for a few minutes and then play or rest. This is critical for quick-maturing puppies. They absorb new skills like sponges, but you have to remember that they are youngsters and need downtime. Older dogs that have a natural work mode will quickly develop the skill. Some dogs develop a work mode quickly during obedience class. Others need help.

If your dog has trouble focusing, you need to build or create focus. Work first in quiet locations, such as your kitchen or garage, and keep other people and pets away. Get your dog's attention by holding a tasty treat and then move around a few small steps. Keep your dog's attention on you with a little voice and a lot of intense attention. Do not continually call your dog's name, just watch him. Move back, forward, and side to side and immediately reward when your dog looks at you and/or follows your motion. Reward your dog *before* he looks away or gets distracted. Keep moving in small steps and keep your dog moving also. Do not use a toy to lure the dog. He will learn to focus on the toy rather than you. Rather, reward focus (looking at you) with a bit of the treat nibbled from your hand. Do not drop the treat for this exercise. Make him nibble from your hand. Work for short durations (a mere minute) and work up to several minutes of intent focus.

> You should continue to use quiet time before and after every training session throughout your dog's competitive career. Training with you will always feel special and fun to your dog.

Once you have focus, add in basic obedience commands such as *Sit, Down, and Wait.* Then work in a mildly distracting environment, such as your own yard or family room with other pets in the room. Continue to reward your dog for focus and vary your rewards. To keep his interest you must be more interesting than the distractions. For high-drive dogs you may need to add more speed to your motions. Finally, work his obedience commands in distracting situations, such as a sidewalk in town, park, or training class. Remember to always reward focus before you lose it.

It is also helpful to give your dog quiet time before and after every training session, regardless of what you are training. Leave your dog alone for a short period before you train. Being alone and then being back with you naturally increases his interest in the training. It also ensures that you are working with a rested, relaxed dog. A short period of rest or quiet time immediately after a training session also helps define the training session. It creates a distinct period of "work" time. With a specific time period devoted to your dog, training seems like playtime to your dog. This is a simple method to keep training sessions fun and interesting.

Off-Leash

Agility is an off-leash sport! Not only does your dog need a work ethic, he must be able to be off-leash and remain in your vicinity. This is frequently referred to as with me. Even beginner exercises require that your dog be controllable without a leash. Once the leash is off, your dog must be workable. He cannot leave, circle, or jump all over you. He cannot run the fence line, choose his own sequences, visit with other dogs, or beg treats from the instructor. These rules apply regardless of whether you are doing agility for fun or competition. This does not mean that your dog has to have an obedience championship before he starts agility! What it means is that your dog is focused on you and will come—immediately—when called.

Furthermore, if you are working in a class situation, your dog should be able to leave other dogs alone. This includes their toys and treats. High-drive dogs can get even higher in class situations. Make sure you have control of and are watching your dog at all times.

Commands Your Dog Needs to Know

SIT

This is your control zone. Your dog should sit on command and should stay put until you release him. With your dog in a reliable sit-stay, you can focus on your instructor, set up a drill, or move away to reset a jump bar or target. Your dog must sit quietly while you are doing something else and while you are holding his collar. Both are critical skills and should be taught immediately, even to young puppies.

DOWN

A drop or down position is used in agility training and is required in some registries on the pause table. Teaching the down position is also an exercise in control. Dogs are reluctant to do a down in strange locations or when there is excessive activity. You should also practice the down on a variety of surfaces, such as carpet, ceramic tile floor, or wet grass. Also do not get in the habit of using your hands to push or encourage your dog into a down. Agility is a hands-free sport!

High-drive dogs need to be under control and willing to wait in a down.

In order to do a down on the pause table, your dog needs to drop without creeping forward. If he creeps forward, he will run out of table. This is particularly true for large breeds, such as Dobermans or Bernese mountain dogs. Furthermore, the down in agility is a moving exercise. Your dog must be able to drop on the table immediately after running to and jumping on the table.

To teach an agility down, ask for a drop while moving. Have your dog do a down while walking next to you (like the moving down station in rally) and then while walking toward you. Once he can drop from a walk, ask for the down from a slow jog, beside you, and then coming toward you. Finally, try for more speed. Remember to keep your dog in the down position for five to ten seconds. It is not drop and go!

WAIT

Agility exercises require a wait or stay. With the dog in a down, stand, or sit, a reliable wait is an absolute must for agility training. You must be able to leave your dog and move away ten to fifteen feet, at least. And your dog must be able to handle distractions, such as another dog trotting by or a toy rolling across the floor. Agility classes and exercises are exciting, which means your dog's wait must be well established. The wait is also "active" in that your dog should be watching you and should be ready to move. It does not mean nap time! Like the sit and down, the wait is an agility exercise that is worked constantly throughout your training, particularly in groundwork and short sequence exercises.

RECALL

Your dog must come when called. His recall must be all the way to you, and he must allow you to get a hold of his collar. A dog that returns to "your vicinity" is not doing a safe recall. Train it and proof it. A reliable recall requires training in different locations and environments over a long period. It is also something that you can continually train. Take half a dozen treats on all your outings and to class. Call your dog back to you at random times and in random situations. This will keep his recall sharp.

RUN TOGETHER

Many agility competitors select dogs from the herding group. Bred for generations to work in teams and to run, these dogs tend to adapt very easily to agility. Whether you own one of these or not, it is vital that your dog be willing to run with you. Running as a team means running at roughly the same pace and in the same direction. As with most skills, some dogs inherently understand this or pick up the concept quickly. Others need help.

Running together is a groundwork skill, but before you can work it into your agility training, your dog must be willing to run along beside you. Test your dog by jogging on a long, straight line. Sidewalks work well. If your dog does not move along briskly with you, lure him along with a favorite toy or tasty treat. Work at a walk and move gradually faster with each training session. Always face forward and keep moving forward and straight. Turning in or running backward facing the dog are body language signals to your dog that mean stay behind me! Offer your dog the reward while you are still moving. Do not throw the reward ahead and do not stop to give him the reward.

RESTRAINED SEND

Another very useful tool in agility training is the restrained send. Many people inadvertently do a restrained send when their dog pulls them down the sidewalk to the park while they chuckle at their dogs' enthusiasm. The dog is pulling forward with drive and desire, but the owner has not yet released the dog. A simple method for teaching the restrained send is to use a treat or toy.

Introduce the Restrained Send

1. With your dog in a stand and your hand holding his collar, throw a favorite treat or toy. Do not throw a treat more than five feet or a toy more than ten feet. Always use a buckle collar for these drills.

2. Wait two or three seconds. Build anticipation with a few words but do not yell. Quiet words infused with your own excitement work best. Let your dog pull you forward slightly. Let him bounce and wiggle. Look for intent focus on the reward.

3. Let go! It is important to let go before your dog settles down or gets discouraged.

4. Once your dog gets his treat or picks up the toy, immediately call the dog back to you for a game of tug or for another treat.

Repeat this simple process five or six times. Think of the restrained send as a game. How much enthusiasm can you build? Can you get a quiet dog to bark with glee? Can you get a timid dog to pull forward a bit? The goal is to teach the dog that a restrained send is fun and that he should stay focused on the object or obstacle in front of him. Timid dogs do not need to leap and pull. They just need to *want* to go forward. Bouncy, high-drive dogs should not be out of control. Pulling a bit is good. Pulling like a sled dog on a moose hunt is unacceptable.

If your dog is reluctant to pull or is put off by your hand in his collar, try a simple variation of the restrained send.

- Hold him with a firm hand on his chest. This often works best for small dogs and puppies. You can also kneel or sit on the floor. Your lowered body position puts you in the game.

- Have a friend hold him while you run away (no more than ten feet). Your dog's reward is to catch you. This works well with puppies. Make sure you do not outrun your dog, and make sure you reward forward motion (keep moving as he catches you). This is also referred to as a restrained recall.

- Let him watch a dog friend play the game, and then let the two dogs race for the reward. Put out or offer two rewards so both dogs can be successful.

Imbedded in the restrained send exercise are three other tools. First, you will immediately learn what your dog loves. What gets him revved up? Is it a specific toy, like a fuzzy snake, tennis ball, or Frisbee? A certain treat? Pay attention to what motivates your dog. Second, you are teaching your dog to focus and move forward. Many of the introduction exercises in this book employ a restrained send to get the dog to move forward with drive. It is a simple bit of reverse psychology.

Most dogs quickly figure out that they want whatever you are holding them back from. And third, you can easily modify the restrained send into a restrained recall. For a restrained recall, have a training partner or your instructor hold the dog. Move forward ahead of the dog and call your dog to you for a reward. Many obedience classes introduce the recall with this method.

PICK UP AND REPOSITION

While this is not necessarily a command, it is well worth teaching your dog to let you pick him up and/or reposition him when necessary. Assuming you do not own a Newfoundland, practice picking up your dog and placing him on the ground, table, or couch. Your dog should remain standing when you put him down. It is also helpful to be able to reposition each foot without having your dog roll over or struggle. We frequently pick up our dogs during contact training, so this is an important skill.

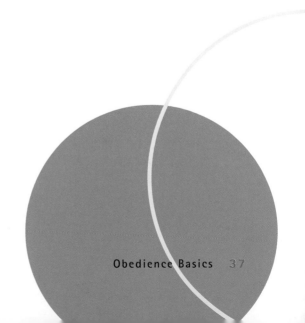

CHAPTER 5

Training ABCs

Animal training is part science and part art. It is both learned and explored. Successful dog trainers work with multiple breeds—from terriers to toys to hounds—and across disciplines—from obedience to herding to skijoring to search and rescue and beyond. They learn from every sport and from every dog. When applied to an individual animal, the knowledge or science of training often becomes an art form, requiring free thinking, problem solving, and a bit of intuition. The basics, however, remain the same.

Classical vs Operant Conditioning

When a dog learns to *associate* an action, place, or event with a pleasant (or unpleasant) consequence, it is classical conditioning. When a dog learns to *offer* a behavior or response intentionally, it is operant conditioning.

In its simplest form, classical conditioning is coincidence or basic survival training. Animals live by the "whatever happens most often is likely to happen again" rule. For example, by the time they are two or three, many dogs associate the smell of a vet's office with shots. The association of discomfort with the vet smell is a classical conditioned response. Your dog learned through trial and error that a visit to the vet is generally not fun. On the other hand, the sound of the can opener usually means dinner, so your dog arrives pronto in the kitchen whenever he hears the can opener. These are examples of reflexive or automatic behavior, rather than intentional behavior.

Almost any behavior response can be modified with careful, steady classical conditioning. One of our students at Mountain Freaks had a dog that was terrified by loudspeakers and ran for his crate every time a sound system squeaked or crackled with static. Since large agility trials frequently use sound systems to convey information and round up volunteers, this was a major problem for the dog and his handler. The solution was to recondition the dog. For several months, we played soft music, then loud music, and then had voices speak on a sound system while they played Frisbee, which is the dog's favorite game. Using classical conditioning we simply changed the dog's association. Today when he hears loud and irregular sounds from a sound system, the dog associates those noises with a game of Frisbee. Not only is he no longer afraid, he is now very vocal and exuberant during loudspeaker announcements.

Intentional behavior occurs when a dog *offers* a behavior to get a response. For example, your dog may scratch at the door when he wants to go outside. He learned through trial and error that scratching receives the desired response of you opening the door. He is intentionally offering the behavior whenever he wants to go outside. Scratching as a means of communication may have started as a reflex behavior—scratching was simply an expression of his impatience—but it evolved into a learned behavior. Whenever you open the door, you reward the offered behavior of scratching. This is operant conditioning. Another common occurrence of operant conditioning is stick retrieving. Every time your dog brings you a stick and you then throw the stick for him to retrieve, you are employing operant conditioning. Your dog offered a behavior (bringing you a stick) and you rewarded (by throwing the stick) his action. Both of these are examples of learned or intentional behaviors.

Think of it this way: When your dog skids into the kitchen when the can opener goes on, he is merely reacting to the sound, gambling that it might be dinnertime. This is classical conditioning. However, if you find him standing on the counter pressing the can opener, he is offering a behavior (deliberately making the can opener sound) for his dinner (the reward). This is an intentional behavior. If you reward him with dinner, then you are using operant conditioning. You will also have a worn-out can opener in a few short weeks!

Training through operant conditioning results in purposeful behavior. Training through classical conditioning results in habitual behavior.

The difference is vast. Dogs trained through operant conditioning *try* to learn new behaviors. And because your dog was aware of the behavior (he thought it out) as he learned, the behavior is sharper and remains for a longer time. With control over the consequences of their actions, dogs become enthusiastic, confident partners. The question frequently becomes: Who is training whom?

GOOD VS BAD ASSOCIATIONS

Associations, particularly in young dogs and puppies, are built continually. A can opener means dinner. A picked-up leash means go for a walk. Tennis balls and Frisbees mean playtime. Walking in wooded areas indicates a good place to hunt squirrels. Walking around a neighborhood means a cat might be around. Most dogs are extremely inquisitive and are willing to explore new environments and situations. Every new encounter or series of encounters builds an association—good or bad. It is your job to monitor your dog's environment to prevent bad or negative associations, and this is particularly true during the introduction to agility equipment.

For young dogs and during early training, the basic rule is: Do not ignore your dog's nerves, even if you think the situation is fine. Avoid training or working your dog in scary situations. And if your dog spooks at a normal object or sound, let him investigate and explore. For example, if a man approaches wearing a big floppy hat that frightens your puppy, let him work his way to the person slowly or have the man gently remove the hat. Let your dog investigate the hat on the ground. A touch of patience can reduce the whole situation to a few moments of humor. Even if your puppy does not build a positive association to a big, floppy hat, he has not built a negative one. For the rest of his life, your dog will simply ignore people wearing big, floppy hats, which is absolutely fine.

Other common environmental problems are barking or whining dogs, clanking metal, clattering PVC poles, whistles, screechy loudspeaker systems, hand clapping and cheering, and blowing, snapping flags or tents. All of these are normal sounds at agility trials. A dog that builds a negative or fear response to any of these will have a difficult time focusing in a competitive environment and may shut-down and refuse to participate. You also want to avoid training around extremely aggressive dogs. Another issue for many dogs is the sound the seesaw makes as it hits the ground, particularly if a sixty-pound dog is riding it down. The *Bang!* spooks many dogs. It sounds like a gunshot or firecracker. When you are waiting for your class to begin, be alert to dogs working on the seesaw or wait to bring your dog into the building until the previous class is finished. At Mountain Freaks we always build a positive association to the sound of the seesaw well before we ask the dog to put his paws on the plank.

You need to be vigilant. Incidents do occur, and you need to rec-ognize them and work—sometimes immediately—to remove negative associations. One day in our novice handling class, a miniature black poodle was running through a jump-tunnel-jump sequence when a rambunctious, tunnel-loving German shepherd decided to sneak in an extra tunnel run while his handler was distracted by a spilled treat bag. Needless to say the little poodle got trampled as the shepherd steamed through the tunnel at full speed. Anticipating that the poo-dle might immediately build a negative association to the tunnel, we had the handler send the dog through the tunnel multiple times and reward with treats and praise lavishly. The poodle had no problems with the tunnel. We all breathed a sigh of relief and resumed training. Curiously, the poodle did build an association. In the following weeks he snarled nastily at every shepherd and shepherd-look-alike in every situation! Months of careful conditioning broke the association down, but his handler is still cautious with his feisty little poodle around shepherds.

Recent research suggests that animals build associations faster and stronger in direct relation to their body's adrenaline response. A highly charged situation, be it from fun or fear, creates an *immediate*, very strong association. This is a basic survival instinct. Adrenaline is a basic component to the "flight or fight" response. It is your job to monitor your dog's environment carefully to prevent negative, fear-induced associations. And always remember that classical and operant conditioning works both ways. Animals constantly learn to avoid and embrace new events and situations.

CLICKERS

A clicker (a small plastic box that makes a "click" noise) makes operant conditioning easier. Clicker training simply uses a specific sound to identify and mark a specific behavior. A quick, efficient click can highlight or mark a specific behavior faster and easier than verbal praise or an offered reward. It also allows the handler to remain quiet and reward from a distance.

As an example, say you want your dog to lie down with his head between his paws. When your dog puts his head down (the desired behavior), how can you reward the offered behavior without drawing his head up? If you offer a reward, your dog receives reinforcement for lifting his head. If you drop a toy, he is rewarded for moving and catching the toy. Of course many, many repetitions may convince him that "head down" is what you want, but there is a shorter path to the desired behavior. A click can mark and reward the head-drop behavior. When his head drops, the click tells him that it was the correct behavior. The treat follows, but it is not what "marked" the behavior.

The time delay—between mark and reward—is critical. It is what makes clicker training so successful. A click tells your dog *exactly* which behavior earned the reward, which he knows will follow. For clicker-trained dogs, a click is great news. It means a reward is coming. They also pay attention and think through which behavior earned the click.

Clicker training is simple, but there are a few rules. First, the click sound can be a click, ding, or chirp but must be consistent and unique. A wide variety of clickers are available from pet stores and training facilities, and they are relatively cheap. Second, whenever you click, you must reward. Clicker training begins with and relies on simple, classical conditioning. Your dog hears a click and associates the sound with a reward. In order to maintain this association, you *must* reward the click. And third, the reward must follow the click in a reasonable timeframe. It does *not* have to be instantaneous, just prompt. And lastly, there is no need to double click. One mark per offered behavior is enough.

The most frequently asked question is why not a word? Compared to a click or chirp, voice praise is not precise, tones change, and volume varies. Furthermore, it is too easy to dilute the association between verbal praise and a reward. Every time your dog hears the verbal mark without a follow-up reward, you are breaking down the association and damaging your communication and training method. At Mountain Freaks we begin with a clicker and then migrate to a verbal mark. This two-phased approach gives the dog time to learn *the process of shaping* with the more concrete sound of a click and encourages the handler to be precise in marking behaviors. We then train a verbal mark for some of the more advanced exercises, such as contact and weave pole work. A verbal mark is necessary in sequence work and under trial conditions to preserve obstacle performance.

Introduce the Click

Before you begin training with a clicker, you must establish the association between the click sound and the reward. This is basic classical conditioning.

1. With your dog in a stand or sit, click.

2. Wait one full second. Do not rush the reward. Give your dog time to absorb the noise.

3. Offer a reward. Small bites of desirable food work best. Remember you are employing classical conditioning. If the drive for the reward is strong, then the association will be strong.

Repeat this simple process five or six times with multiple variations. You want your dog to understand that it is the click that provides the reward, not where you are or how you and he are positioned.

- After every other click, change the way you offer the reward. Switch hands. Visibly toss or drop the treat on the floor. If you always offer the reward from the right hand, after several repetitions your dog will search for your hand when he hears the click. Remember, classical conditioning is a strong tool.

You must be careful what association is being built. You want "click equals reward" not "click equals find my right hand"!

- Shift your position. Stand up or kneel. Move one step away from your dog. Sit in a chair.

- Move to a different location. Change rooms or go outside/inside.

Before you use a verbal mark, you must repeat the above exercise with the verbal instead of the click sound. At Mountain Freaks we like to use a brisk happy "Yes!" We also intermittently reinforce the association ("Yes!" equals reward).

Shaping

Shaping is a training technique by which a subject (aka your dog) is reinforced for offering closer and closer approximations to a desired behavior. It is operant conditioning fine-tuned. Shaping makes teaching new behaviors easier, and it is particularly effective when training an unnatural behavior, such as pressing a can opener or weaving. There are very few dogs that, upon sighting twelve white poles in a straight line and separated by less than two feet, would decide to weave at full speed between the poles!

Shaping (aka operant conditioning) focuses the trainer's and dog's attention on positive behavior. It recognizes and rewards progress and keeps training sessions fun through positive reinforcement. Each incremental improvement in the offered behavior is rewarded until the target behavior is achieved. This technique has several key concepts. First, the behavior or piece of the behavior must be offered by the dog. Second, the dog must desire the reinforcement or reward. And third, the final behavior must be clearly understood or visualized by the trainer. In order for shaping to be successful, it is important to *clearly* define the objective or target behavior. The trainer must know when to mark. Timing is everything.

It is also important to know when to withhold reinforcement. Receiving a mark tells the dog that the last action was correct. Not receiving a mark also tells the dog something, and frequently it is the nonresponse that is clearer. For example, if you want to teach your dog to drop his head and keep it on his paws, he must be rewarded when his head is down. If he puts his head down between his paws for a mere second, then he is offering a head dip. In order to get the head down for a longer period, you withhold the mark for longer and longer periods until his head stays down. It is your nonresponse to the head dip that clarifies for your dog which behavior you truly want.

HOW IT WORKS

Shaping a behavior is a process. Simple actions—such as shake paw—have a concrete, easily visualized target behavior and simple intermediate steps. Complex actions—such as weaving—are a composite of actions and require multiple, complex intermediate steps.

The Process	Simple Example
Step 1 Define the behavioral objective. Picture the complete, successful behavior. You must have a specific, concrete idea and target behavior. Picture the end result. Be specific. Decide whether the behavior is cued verbally or thru motion.	Behavior: Shake paw Mental picture: • right paw • dog in a sit in front of handler • verbal cue is "shake" • physical cue is hand out flat.
Step 2 Assess the dog's current skill set. Determine how much your dog already knows. Has the behavior been offered? Is it a natural behavior or learned?	Offered behavior: no Applicable skills: • very nose oriented • is food motivated and frantic about steak or roast beef

Step 3

Determine the steps needed for the behavior. Use the dog's present skill level and work forward to the target behavior. What intermediate steps are necessary to get from the current state to final? How many skills does the dog need? What order should the skills be taught?

Action plan:
1. Sit front
2. Wait
3. Offer paw
4. Shake

Existing skills:
- sit front
- wait with attention
- clicker trained
- allows paws to be held without pulling backward

Step 4

Break the target behavior into steps. Each step, stage, or goal must be attainable, and it must be a *logical* progression from the previous step. In other words, it must be a behavior your dog can logically offer. Use lots of positive reinforcement for each step toward the desired behavior.

Step summary: Use small pieces of steak in closed fist to encourage paw scraping, then use curled fingers over treat to get paw scrape, and then open palm to get paw touch. Hold paw and shake.

Specifics:
With dog in a sit in front of handler and allowing dog to see treat going into hand:
1. Close fist. Get paw scrape at closed fist. Reward.
2. Hide treat under curled fingers. Get paw scrape to open fingers. Reward.
3. Curl fingers (no treat). Get paw scrape to open fingers. Reward.
4. Open palm (no treat). Get paw placed on hand. Reward.
5. Open palm extended. Get paw on hand. Close fingers on paw. Shake. Reward.

Step 5	Example:
Shape each step or stage. Elicit the desired behavior and reward. Reinforce each effort. The level of skill should be progressively more demanding. Remember: Shaping works by rewarding behaviors that come closer and closer to the preset goal. As skills are built or mastered, the dog is rewarded for improvement. Once the dog has mastered a specified behavior, he must offer the next stage of behavior in order to receive another reward. Constant reinforcement helps new behaviors become established.	The goal is to get a paw scrape on your closed fist. • mark and reward a lifted paw • mark and reward any touch of paw on your body or arm • mark and reward paw touch on hand • mark and reward paw scrape at hand Note: Not every dog goes through every step, and every dog progresses at a different rate. These variations make shaping a bit of an art form.
Step 6	Physical cue: hand extended
Attach a cue to the desired behavior. As each step is achieved, the target behavior is shaped but only the final behavior receives a cue, which can be a verbal or physical signal or both.	Verbal cue: *Shake*

DISENGAGE

Another key concept to shaping is the "disconnect." When the dog offers an inappropriate or unwanted behavior, the handler disconnects or disengages by looking away for a short period (seconds not minutes). Look at the ceiling, clouds, or in the opposite direction from the dog. This is a *neutral* response. It is neither negative nor positive. A neutral response tells the dog that the behavior is not being accepted without being a correction. Disengaging also offers the dog time to think and offer another behavior. Be patient. Give your dog time to think through the process and offer the behavior.

JACKPOT

Frequently it is after one of these pauses—or thinking spots—that an animal offers the next behavior. When this happens, trainers use a jackpot. Typically the dog receives one reward per marked behavior. However, dogs do occasionally leap forward through the process or have a breakthrough moment. To reward this fast-forward progression, or leap, mark and offer multiple rewards and extensive verbal praise. This is referred to as a "jackpot." Do not mark or click multiple times. The behavior is marked once but rewarded with a jackpot. The jackpot highlights the desired behavior. It can also be used to reward a particularly sharp effort or a behavior that took multiple tries to obtain. A jackpot tells the dog, "Yes! Yes! That was it!"

Whenever possible you also want to end all your training session on a "jackpot moment."

The Process of Shaping

Animal trainers use shaping to teach new behaviors, but shaping is also a learned process—for both the trainer and the animal. Marking the exact behavior and knowing how to wait for an incremental change takes practice. It is a learned skill. Choose a simple behavior for your first attempt, such as paw shake, nose touch on your hand, lip lick, or paw touch on a pad. Once you have perfected the reinforcement process (marking and rewarding incremental behavior changes), shaping a specific behavior is easier.

However, shaped behaviors are well learned and difficult to break or change. Be very, very careful what behavior you are shaping and watch carefully for imbedded (unwanted) behaviors. For instance, if you are training your dog to shake paw, make sure he does not bark or sneeze or stand up before offering a paw. It is shockingly easy to end up with a shake paw command that has a bark before the shake.

Keep in mind also that dogs *learn* the process too. Dogs that have been through the shaping process a few times understand "reward for a new behavior" and frequently begin to offer new behaviors on their own and at a faster rate. They also offer different behaviors when a reward is withheld. Once you teach your dog to think independently, you cannot expect him to think creatively on command. Once he understands shaping, your dog will *think* through every training process. Be aware of offered behaviors. Many trainers get frustrated with a dog that continually offers new behaviors. Frustration is the fastest path to a team breakdown.

After you teach your dog to "think," you have to think harder and faster than he does! Keep your reactions neutral and analyze the behavior or lack of behavior. Break down the steps when necessary to ensure clarity. For instance, during a short sequence drill, you want your dog to turn left as he jumps through the tire. If he turns right or continues straight, you do not reward his leap through the tire. However, a dog that understands shaping also understands that he is wrong after several repetitions without a reward. So, he stops offering the tire jump. He may suddenly go under the tire, or he may run off and do a tunnel, which even if it is a long shot for a reward, at least it is fun! Your dog is offering alternate behaviors. Since you taught him to do this, your response at this point is critical. Anger and frustration break down trust. When your dog does something "off the wall," remind yourself that your dog is thinking creatively.

FIX A BREAKDOWN

So how do you fix the breakdown? Use your training and communication skills to clarify your desires. The solution is to break down the required behavior. If your dog is offering alternate behaviors, he is still engaged and trying. Make it easier and let him be successful. Shift the creative thinking burden to yourself.

1. Take a short break to regroup. Offer your dog a drink and take time to think.

2. Mark the original (or last offered) behavior again to establish your base. Let your dog know that the behavior was correct (i.e., mark two successful tire jumps regardless of the landing).

3. Change the format. Make it easier for your dog to offer the behavior. For example, you can move the dog closer to the jump or alter his approach angle to ensure a left turn. You can also break down the task into smaller increments (ignore the tire jump for a few minutes and get your dog to follow your body cues through a left turn on the flat). You should also consider the environment. For instance, try the same drill on a bar jump. The problem could be a flaw in your dog's initial training to always jump the tire jump straight.

INTERMITTENT REINFORCERS

In order to maintain the desired behavior once it is established, use an intermittent reinforcer. Mark and reward every third, fourth, or fifth time the behavior is offered. As the behavior becomes established, the reinforcer can be offered randomly, but it must continue to be offered.

REWARDS

An intrinsic part of shaping—or any other positive reinforcement training—is the reward. A reward is something given in return for service or action. It is the payment! Dogs, like people, have preferences. A Border collie may want to chase and retrieve a tennis ball, a terrier may want to play a feisty game of tug with a squeaky toy, and a golden retriever may want a hunk of string cheese. Knowing which payment your dog prefers is a major component of positive reinforcement. Also remember to vary your rewards. Switch from hot dogs to chicken to cheese or switch from a squeaky to a fuzzy tug every few training sessions. You can also up the ante. If you are working your dog with more distractions or your dog is having a difficult time with a drill, change the treat to something really desirable. If you typically use hot dogs, switch to roast beef or steak. Your dog must desire the reward in order to offer the behavior. Keep it interesting and fun.

Treats are preferred for shaping exercises. Toys and tug games interrupt the flow of the exercise. Teachers do not let their students jump up and run around the classroom halfway through a math problem. Their students would lose the flow and forget what they were doing. Remember shaping is a *thinking* exercise for your dog, like math is to humans. Unless you can satisfy your dog with a very brief tug, do not use a toy when shaping a behavior for the first time. If your dog is not food driven, put your training sessions in front of mealtimes to ensure that he is hungry.

It is also important to have a variety of rewards. Several of the advanced drills for contact and weave training use a toy. If your dog is not naturally into toys, now is the time to develop toy drive. There are several easy ways to do this. First, use a soft toy that makes a noise that your dog finds interesting or a fuzzy one that he can chase. Take your dog shopping! What attracts your dog's attention? Test a variety of toys and noises to see which one makes your dog perk up. For little dogs check out the cat toys, too. Second, use the

Also keep in mind that training provides dogs with lots of extra food, particularly when shaping complex behaviors. You may need to reduce your dog's meal portions on training days. Furthermore, always bring your dog to class hungry. You want him motivated to work, so do not feed your dog a meal in the hours before class or a training session.

new, fascinating toy to play. Set up playtime sessions for early morning or when you get home from work. This is when your dog is happy to see you. Get down on the floor and bat the toy around, squeak it, hide it, toss it in the air . . . just play with the toy. During playtime do not carry or offer treats; make the toy the reward.

Another useful method to engage your dog is to play with another dog. A little jealousy goes a long way. Let your dog watch you play with another dog, preferably a toy-obsessed dog. When playing with another dog, simply ignore your dog. Lavishly praise the dog with the toy and enjoy yourself. Leave a few extra toys around on the floor and let your dog pick one out to offer you. If your dog brings you a toy, play sporadically with both dogs but do not let the dogs play with each other.

If your dog is still reluctant to play, try a soft toy or tennis ball with treats inside. There are a variety of toys on the market that have built-in food pouches.

ACCURACY EVALUATION

Whenever you are shaping a behavior, you must constantly evaluate the degree of accuracy. How frequently is your dog performing the desired behavior? Good trainers think in terms of numbers not just vague phrases like "most," "some," or "only a few." Evaluate your dog's performance as a percent. For example, if he waits on a lead-out nine out of ten times, you have a lead-out 90 percent of the time. If your dog only waits five out of ten times, you only have a lead-out 50 percent of the time. The ability to objectively measure your dog's performance is a critical skill. Don't guess. Keep track in your head, have a training partner count for you, or write it down.

You must also be objective in analyzing accuracy as an independent behavior. How much did you have to support your dog's effort? For example, your dog did nine out of ten waits at the start line. However, if he scooted forward once and you actually asked him to sit back down once, then your percentage is off. Objectively, your dog waited seven out of ten times. You must continue to evaluate your dog's performance against the ideal. Do not lower your expectations. Alter your reward schedule or training method—not your expectation.

The next step is to decide how much is enough to move on. We like to see *at least* an 80 percent success rate before we change the difficulty of a drill or exercise. So the phrase "with success" or "consistently successful" means you are getting a solid, independent performance eight out of ten tries. Do not count mediocre behaviors and do not demand 110 percent perfection. Both are hard on your canine teammate.

Corrections

At Mountain Freaks, agility training is a process. Each step builds gently on the next. The basic training skills in this chapter are used throughout the equipment introduction and groundwork phases. The skills learned in the groundwork drills are used extensively in the short sequence work. And the techniques taught during short sequence work are the foundation for course work. Each layer makes the transition to the next easier and smoother. It is this cohesive system that creates a dynamic team.

Training with positive reinforcement and simple shaping makes success attainable for every dog and handler team. Every new task is presented simply and easily. Your dog can offer the behavior. Nothing is forced. Agility is an off-leash sport. You cannot make your dog perform, and you cannot force your dog to run with you. It is an equal partnership. The Mountain Freaks methodology introduces every piece of equipment in logical steps to allow your dog to learn without pressure. Keeping it simple is a rule. It also keeps your communication with your dog clear and concise. Verbal cues reinforce physical cues and physical cues do not contradict each other. With clarity, dogs learn faster and transition quicker.

TWO STRIKES RULE

From equipment training to full course work, we use a two strikes rule. Basically this says you and your dog get two tries to succeed. If the first attempt is unsuccessful, try again. If the second attempt is successful, reward it and move on. If the second attempt is not a complete success, then you must stop and alter the format, complexity, and/or environment of the exercise.

For example, if your dog misses a weave pole entry from an angled tunnel, then you would stop and remain neutral for a couple seconds or until the dog settles down. A neutral response lets your dog know that the behavior was unacceptable. Then loop back and try the tunnel-weave combination again. This is the second attempt. If the dog succeeds, reward the weave poles and continue the sequence. If he fails again, stop! Begin training for success. In this example, you should give another neutral response for several seconds and then put the dog at the tunnel exit and send him to the weaves. If he succeeds, try the tunnel-weave sequence again. If he fails, put him halfway between the tunnel and the weaves. If he succeeds, put him at the tunnel exit and try again. If he fails from halfway between the obstacles, then take the dog back to the same spot you just attempted and gently lead him through the poles with a hand in his collar. There should be no mark or treat this time, since you are doing the work. Then reattempt from the same angle, this time letting the dog go on his own. The point is that for every failure there is a subtle change in the format of the exercise. With another failure from midway between the tunnel and weaves, you must change another criterion. You could open the weave poles or reduce the angle.

After two strikes you must back up through your training until you have success and then step forward through each step that you progressed backward. Do not move forward until you have success. Reward each success that the dog offers.

EMBEDDED CORRECTIONS

Another primary piece of the Mountain Freak's training system is embedded corrections. By using a systematic, consistent approach to introduce, train, and proof the obstacles, we minimize errors and train the correction into the learning process. For example, the introduction to the dog walk is done with the handler using a restrained send down the *last four feet* of the board to the target. This is also a correction for a missed zone in sequence training.

There are multiple benefits to embedded corrections. First, the correction is clearly understood by the dog. It was part of his training on the equipment from day one. And because it was part of the introduction, the correction is not negative. It is a clarification. Second, communication between dog and handler is always clear. The dog knows what the handler is doing and what is expected. The correction is gentle. And third, with the correction learned during the introduction, it is a habit, particularly for the handler. With the correction for an error clearly defined, the handler already has the tool needed to fix the problem—immediately. Knowing how to clarify your desires to your dog makes training smoother and easier.

Targets

A target is a training tool used to focus the dog's attention to a specific area. In agility the *target* area is usually down, such as at the end of the dog walk or A-frame, or forward, such as at the end of a tunnel. The actual target is an object that is placed on the ground. It can be a plastic lid, a small square of plexiglass, a ceramic tile, an extra piece of board, or a foam mat. It should be visible to the dog and should be an object the dog will not try to pick up. For the first month, use the same target for your training. After a few weeks most dogs can generalize the target behavior to a variety of objects. It is also useful to use a target that can be cut down or reduced in size, which is particularly important in the contact training sequence.

A target is used to induce a specific behavior. The Mountain Freaks methodology uses target training in multiple exercises. It is a powerful tool that is self-reinforcing (aka a positive motivator). It is taught as a game and is fun for the dogs. For example, below are two basic behaviors trained with targets. Both are explained in detail in later chapters.

1. A run ahead or go forward. This is a key behavior for teaching independent weave poles, tunnel sends, and a rear-cross.

2. A stay or wait at the bottom of the yellow zone on a contact.

Target training employs both classical and operant conditioning. The first step is to build the association between the target and the reward. Using classical conditioning we teach the dog that the target object is a food dispenser. This is the dog's rule: The target object equals food. The goal is to get the dog to focus and move independently forward. During target training it is important that the dog learns to drive to the target. Enthusiasm and focus are critical components.

The final step, using operant conditioning, modifies the drive forward behavior into an offered wait. In order to get the dog to offer a wait, we build in an intermediate step, typically a nose or paw touch. The target touch, whether it is a nose touch or paw touch, gives the dog something to do. Once the dog is doing or offering a behavior at the target, you can begin shaping the wait. Remember: With operant conditioning, you cannot shape the behavior unless it is offered.

Thus the entire target training process has several intermediate steps.

Step 1: Introduce the Target

Step 2: Shape the Target Touch

Step 3: Run to the Target

Step 4: Shape the Wait

The poodle is in a 2-foot-on, 2-foot-off wait on the dog walk.

INTRODUCE THE TARGET

Target introduction is best done in a quiet location and when your dog is hungry. The goal of this exercise is to simply teach the dog that the target equals food. Find the target . . . find the food.

1. Hold the target in the palm of your left hand, directly in front of you. You can sit or kneel on the ground next to your dog for the introduction. Hold your dog at your side in a restrained send.

> **Trouble Shooting:** If the dog does not look at the target or try to sniff it, move your hand holding the target to focus his attention. Do not use a specific verbal cue. Look at the target, not the dog.

2. Release your dog and mark (click) the dog's connection to the target.

3. Repeat again with the left hand and then switch to holding the target in the right hand for several reps.

Once your dog is sniffing the target, try holding the target in different positions, such as farther away (arm extended) or higher or lower. The next step is to get the target onto the floor. Hold the target in your hand and lower your hand to the floor. With a successful target touch, place the target directly on the floor. You can gently tap the target or toss it gently on the floor to focus your dog's attention. Never put a treat directly on the target. Your dog must offer the target touch, even if it takes a few tries to shape the behavior.

The next step is to fine-tune this interest in the target into a specific touch. It does not matter whether your dog offers a nose or paw touch. Some dogs are foot-oriented and immediately offer a paw touch, particularly once the target is on the ground. Go with whatever your dog offers first. You must be consistent however. If your dog offers a paw touch and you mark (click and reward) the behavior, you cannot change to a nose touch after a few repetitions.

SHAPE THE TARGET TOUCH

For purposes of this explanation, a nose touch is used. If your dog offers a paw touch, be careful to shape a true paw touch. *Picture your dog's paw on the target.* It is a paw or paws pressing down or scrapping at the target. Also remember that not every dog needs every incremental step. If your dog offers the behavior, mark it and reward it! Place the target directly on the floor in front of you. You should kneel or sit for this exercise.

1. Hold the dog in a restrained send with the target a few feet away. Release the dog to the target. Do not use a verbal cue.

> **Trouble Shooting** If your dog turns its back to you, try again with a shorter distance or toss the target forward to get your dog's focus. Keep the treats out of sight and minimize your hand motions.

2. Mark the dog's head motion down (or foot touch) at the target. *Always reward by placing the treat on the target—never*

feed from your hand. If you feed from your hand, your dog will very quickly treat your hand as a target.

Repeat the sequence again and remember to raise the criteria for a reward with each repetition. The desired behavior is a nose touch on the target. At this stage do not reward vague head bobs or a neutral stand in the vicinity of the target. Look for (picture in your head) a nose touch.

This is where you should add a verbal command. Common choices are *Touch, Hit It,* or *Target.*

Once your dog is reliably pulling to the target and offering a target touch, move back two dog lengths and repeat the exercise. Continue using a restrained send. After your dog is offering a deliberate nose touch from a distance, stand up and repeat the exercise. Do not point or move to the target. It is important that you remain stationary. Your dog should be sending to the target not moving with you.

Basic target shaping should be done over the course of a week or two. Break the training sessions into short periods over several days to keep your dog's interest high. He should also be hungry and interested in training. Use quiet time before and after each training session. Most dogs learn quickly that the target means food, but you should continue to use a very desirable food, no toys.

RUN TO TARGET

Your next goal is to get your dog to drive forward to the target from a distance of ten to fifteen feet. For this exercise hold your dog in a restrained send but remain stationary. It is important at this stage of the training that the handler not move. Send your dog and let him offer the touch on the target. If you walk toward the target with your dog, you are directing not shaping. It is the equivalent of picking up your dog's paw for a shake paw. The dog did what you wanted, but it was not an *offered* behavior. If you find yourself inching forward or leaning toward the target, place a piece of tape or a bar on the ground to keep your position stationary. Make this a game and work when your dog is interested in food and attention.

1. With the target a foot or two in front of you, release your dog to the target.

2. Mark the target touch and reward with a treat on the target.

3. Every few successful target touches, move back one foot. Continue to use a restrained send. Mark only deliberate target touches, not a pass over or vague touch.

Gradually increase the distance to the target. Move back in one-foot increments. Be careful to remain stationary until your dog reaches the target. As the distance to the target increases, you can have a training partner put the treat on the target or you can toss the treat onto the target.

Training Tip

During the initial training some dogs will not race to the target. Every dog learns at a different pace. Do not try to force speed. Watch instead for focus and a straight line from you to the target. Many of the advanced drills for contact training will help build drive. For now try jazzing up your restrained send or change to a more desirable treat.

SHAPE THE WAIT

The final step is to shape the target touch into a wait. A dog that understands *touch the target* should offer the behavior until it is rewarded. For the final step you simply wait and let your dog offer multiple touches before you mark the behavior. For example, mark one touch then ask for two touches on the next rep.

For purposes of this explanation, a nose touch is used. However, at this stage a dog that understands shaping frequently offers multiple behaviors. He may offer a nose touch, a sit, a paw touch, or a down. Do not discourage your dog from offering different behaviors, just do

Paw touches are perfectly acceptable, but your dog must wait.

not mark them. Be careful to reinforce only one touch behavior. It is the wait at the target—after the touch—that you are now shaping and that you will need later. By increasing the number of touches before the mark, you increase the time your dog waits at the target. Make this a game!

1. Hold the dog in a restrained send with the target one dog length away. Release your dog to the target.

2. Wait! Mark the dog's *second* nose touch. Reward on the target.

3. Send again and mark the *first* nose touch. Reward on the target.

4. Send again and wait! Mark the dog's *third* nose touch. Reward on the target.

With each rep ask for a different number of nose touches, up to five. And remember you are shaping a wait at target, so do not mark if your dog is not at the target.

Target foundation training is important for contact training. The advanced target training in Contact Obstacles (chapter 9) expands on these exercises. Work these exercises to ensure that your dog fully understands the wait at the target. This is an important prerequisite to combining the target with another piece of equipment.

CHAPTER 6

Groundwork

Before, after, and between every jump, tunnel, or contact obstacle, there is space—twelve, fifteen, or even twenty feet of *ground*. A typical agility course with twenty obstacles has twenty-two sections of ground. Even a short, four-obstacle sequence has six distinct spaces: one before the first obstacle, four between the obstacles, and one at the end. It is across these spaces—between the obstacles—that an agility team shows off their communication and teamwork. Groundwork is the foundation of agility teamwork and, as such, it is trained first, before the dog begins training on the equipment.

On a competition agility course, every dog climbs the A-frame, but only some dogs approach the obstacle with speed and confidence and are ready to immediately zoom off to the next obstacle. How does the handler communicate with her dog? How does she direct a dog traveling almost twelve-miles-per-hour past two jumps, up the A-frame, and then back through a twisty tunnel? How does the dog know her handler is going to turn right after the A-frame–tunnel sequence? Why does the last dog spin before the tire jump, while her dog flies confidently through and across the finish line?

Every successful agility team relies on a fluid language between dog and handler. The subtle communication of motion, attention, and focus between canine and human is exciting and intriguing. The teamwork of a fast, furious run is inspiring. It is what makes agility interesting for the dogs and us.

Teamwork is also possible for every agility team regardless of the speed at which the team works or what level they are training.

Teamwork begins with a simple buildup of communication skills. Equivalent to vocabulary words, this basic language allows the dog

Clear communication between the obstacles makes great teamwork. (Photo courtesy of Joe Canova)

and handler to begin functioning as a coordinated team. Each member balances and reads the other. Successful handlers do not just direct the dog from obstacle to obstacle. They flow with their partner on an agility course. They move and shift as their canine partner moves and adjusts to their motion and commands.

The dynamics required—even in a short agility sequence—necessitate that the handler clearly communicate intent, direction, and speed to the dog. The actual obstacle performance, once trained, becomes instinctive. If you can direct your dog to the A-frame, then he will climb the A-frame. If there is a miscommunication and your dog spins before the A-frame, he looses momentum, which affects his ability to complete the obstacle. If you lose your connection completely and your dog takes the tunnel, then his ability to do the A-frame is no longer important. With a solid communication system in place, your ability to get your dog to the correct obstacle increases and his confidence in you as his teammate improves immeasurably. It is this confidence and trust that makes a successful agility team.

At the root of teamwork is respect and rock-solid understanding. At Mountain Freaks the foundation of this communication is taught away from the jumps, tunnels, and contacts. The basics are taught on the "flat" or "ground" and are referred to as "groundwork." Without equipment there are no zones to worry about, no bars to knock, no entries to miss. It is purely dog and handler. Teammates are able to focus on each other and be successful. Teaching groundwork and teamwork away from the obstacles also encourages smoothness and forces the handler to be precise in his directions and rewards.

Building on the basic obedience commands, agility groundwork uses five commands: *Wait, Close, Out, Back,* and *Go.* These are movement-oriented commands (versus obstacle performance commands like *Jump* or *Seesaw*) and build or refine on the dog and handler's ability to function together.

Groundwork is the foundation beneath agility teamwork. Motion commands allow the handler to effectively position the dog for the next obstacle or series of obstacles. They tell the dog where to go and also where the handler is going. The quick, simple flow of information learned in these groundwork sequences—and then built into short sequence training—allows the dog to perform obstacles with confidence.

> **Training Tip**
>
> All the groundwork exercises assume that the dog already knows sit and down and wait and has a reliable come. Each of these four simple obedience commands should be worked each week, and positive behavior should be reinforced continually.

Another vital component of groundwork training is the handler's ability to keep an eye on the dog. Your dog must focus on the equipment, but you must focus on your dog. If you look at the equipment or check your position, you are dropping your connection to your dog. This is similar to a dead zone in cell phone coverage. Your dog is left with no information. It is the equivalent of the "Hello! Are you there?" of a dropped cell phone call. On an agility course your dog is totally reliant on you to provide instructions. Most dogs do not read the numbers, though some seasoned competition dogs make very logical guesses! If you are not watching your dog, you cannot provide information in a timely manner. During the groundwork exercises, practice keeping your eyes on your dog. The position of the handler in these drills allows for a solid, steady connection (eyes and hand) between dog and handler.

Wait

One of the first commands taught in obedience, puppy, or pet-handling class is *Stay* or *Wait*. This simple command gives the dog owner control over his dog. Although agility does not use a formal stay, the wait command is in constant use. The difference between wait and stay is two-fold. A stay does not require that the dog be focused on the handler, and the handler typically returns to the dog. With a wait, the dog is required to watch the handler and must be ready to move. Wait is the same whether the dog is sitting, standing, in a down, outside the ring, or on a contact obstacle.

A reliable, well-proofed wait is a prerequisite to all agility work. Your dog must be able to sit, focused on you, at a minimum distance of ten feet before you begin agility training. The following exercises are intended to fine-tune this basic training.

THE RELEASE

Staring intently at the handler, ready and eager to move, the dog must wait until he is told to move. But when? Should the dog move when the handler looks at him? How about when the handler says his name? Should the dog move forward when the handler raises an arm? What if the handler stops and then moves forward again? Was that the signal?

The first rule in teamwork is never make your partner guess! The dog's job is to wait for the appropriate signal to move. The handler's job is to always give the appropriate signal. In agility this signal is the release word. A release word is a simple verbal command that gives your dog permission to move. *Okay* is a popular choice. Other options are *Free, Start,* or *Ready.*

A short word is always best, because a release is often followed by another command. For example, from the pause table, the handler may

Waiting for a formal release is a critical skill.

say, "Okay. Tunnel." These two commands: (1) release the dog from the table and (2) send him forward to the tunnel. However, if the handler uses "Alright, let's go!" as a release, then the dog is momentarily directionless while he listens for the next command. He may slow down or he may simply guess what the handler intends him to do after the table. "Alright, let's go! Tunnel!" just takes too long to say.

In every agility exercise and for every situation, the release word is the same.

The timing of the release is critical. The verbal release *Okay* is always given before the handler goes into motion. In other words, the release is not forward motion. It is a word, a verbal command for action. In advanced competition work the handler may go into motion as the verbal command is given, because fractions of a second count.

Okay is also not *Go* or *Come*. A *Go* command sends the dog ahead of the handler, while *Come* calls the dog to the handler. *Come* also ends with dog and handler stationary. In most agility drills and short sequences, you do not want your dog to stop nor cut in front of you. More often you want the dog at your side so you can move together toward the next obstacle. Using *Come* to mean two things, "come front" and "come with me" dilutes the meaning of both. And ambiguity damages the fabric of your team's language. *Come* is also not a release. When recalling the dog, an agility handler will typically say, "Okay. Come."

Introduce a Release

1. Select a release word.

2. Hold dog in a restrained send. [See pages 35–37] Roll a toy or treat a short distance in front of you across the floor.

3. Say the release word and then let go of the dog. The verbal command must precede the release action. This builds an association: release word equals okay to move forward.

4. Repeat five or six times.

5. With dog in a sit, move three feet forward and face away from the dog. Look back at your dog by turning your shoulders slightly. Connect with hand and eyes. Say the release word. Encourage his motion forward by moving forward yourself *after* the dog moves. Reward with treat or toy when your dog catches up to you.

PRACTICE DRILLS

With your dog in a sit, move forward five to ten feet and face away from him. Select one or two of the following practice drills and determine the ratio you want to release the dog versus asking him to wait. The reward schedule for wait is important. For example, if your dog has a difficult time waiting, then you should reward his wait three times for every one release. If your dog has a solid wait, you can reward the wait once for every two releases. Regardless of how rock solid you think his wait is trained, always remember to reward the wait occasionally and keep it active (focused on you).

- Move forward two feet. Stop. Move forward another two feet. Stop. Keep your eyes on your dog. Release.

- Move briskly away. Stop. Connect with hand and eyes. Release.

- Move sidewise to the dog. Connect with hand and eyes. Release.

- Move forward five feet. Stop and pretend to retie your shoe-lace. Stand up. Connect with hand and eyes. Release.

- Walk in a circle around the dog before moving forward a few feet. Connect with hand and eyes. Release.

- Actively use a wrong word (e.g., "Noodle!"). Return to the dog and reward if he does not move. If he moves, gently put back. Soften the word the next time.

ANTICIPATION PROBLEMS

Anticipation can be an agility handler's worst enemy. For many exercises, and for a high percentage of sequence drills, the handler leads out (moves in front of the dog) and releases the dog to him. The constant repetition of lead-out (moving ahead of the dog on a start line or sequence) and release builds excitement and anticipation and, as the dog gets more experience, he anticipates and releases himself. As the dog gets more reliable, the handler may become sloppy in timing the release word with forward motion. Since motion is a stronger cue than a verbal one, the dog begins to release on motion or suggestion of motion rather than waiting for the verbal.

The solution to these very common problems is to train and ask for different behaviors from the dog on the start line or at any other stop point, such as the pause table or bottom of a contact. Before you begin working with agility equipment, you can test and proof your dog's commitment to wait and begin to train a variety of behaviors with a groundwork lead-out. With your dog in a sit, move forward and face him. Vary the distance from five to twenty-five feet. Vary your location: face dog, face away from dog, or move to the side. Remember to reward the wait and the alternate behavior.

- Ask dog to speak.

- Get dog to do a simple trick such as wave paw, lick lips, or shake his head.

- Throw a toy or treat back at the dog to catch. Before you throw the toy or treat, say, "Okay. Catch." This helps your dog understand that he can move to catch it. If your dog does not know how to catch a reward, train it before you use it in a drill. Be careful to always throw the toy or treat at the dog. If he misses the treat, it should land at his paws or behind him; never throw short. If your dog thinks he needs to move forward to catch his toy or treat, you will be adding to his anticipation problem.

- Ask dog to lie down or stand using a hand or verbal signal.

- Put your dog in a sit and walk in a circle around him. This reminds your dog that he cannot move—even though you moved—until released. Every other circle, release your dog on alternating sides of your circle.

Close

The purpose of this command is to get the dog to return to the handler's side. It pulls the dog back into the handler's space. The dog should also be ready for the next signal. An important part of a close is to ensure that the dog does not pass the handler's leg and remains on a parallel or converging path to the handler. At the completion of a close, your dog's spine should be parallel to your body. It is similar to the obedience heel position. However, a close is done on both the right and left sides and the dog's focus point is the handler's hand and/or motion. For groundwork exercises the dog should be locked onto the handler's hand and focused on the path.

For agility training one word is used for both the left and right side, since the dog's response to the hand signal is the same on both sides. The *Close* command also keeps the dog focused on the handler's hand signals. In a sequence where the handler changes sides, this is critical. Before working the *Close* command, your dog needs to understand that he should follow and pay attention to your hand.

FOLLOW THE HAND DRILLS—BASIC

The following exercises are fun, fast drills to teach your dog to chase your hand and to focus on a hand switch (left-to-right or right-to-left). Do not use a toy for these drills. The dog may end up chasing and following the toy versus your hand. It is also helpful to use a soft treat that your dog can nibble whenever he "catches" your hand. You do not want to drop the treat. It must come from your hand.

Hand Tap

With the dog sitting at your right side, place a large visible treat between your fingers. Hold your hand directly over dog's nose and encourage him to stretch upward to sniff or take the treat. Mark each attempt and let your dog stretch higher or leap up to get the treat. Mark any motion upward. Slowly increase the distance between your dog and hand with each repetition. Once your dog is actively reaching up or jumping up to touch your hand, use smaller and less visible treats.

Stretching

Stand or sit your dog between your feet. Place your left hand on his chest. With a treat in the right hand, lure your dog's nose around your right leg. Do not let the dog move forward. Gently stretch the dog's neck around your right leg and then switch hands and repeat on the left. Do not force your dog's head around. Entice him with a treat.

Figure Eight around Legs

The figure eight teaches the dog to follow a simple hand switch: right-to-left or left-to-right. Always use one, fairly large treat and switch the treat from your right hand to your left or vice versa. After multiple repetitions, your dog should follow your hand through a full rotation before receiving a reward. Speed is not necessary. Since you use both hands in this exercise, it is not possible to click. Use the treat alone to reward effort.

Stand your dog between your feet. With a treat in the right hand, lure the dog's nose around your right leg and allow him to follow your hand. When your dog's nose is behind your right knee, switch the treat from your right hand into your left and lure the dog forward. Reward. With treat in your left hand, lure the dog around your left leg. When your dog's nose is behind your left knee, switch the treat from your left hand into your right and draw the dog forward. Reward. As you work this exercise, alternate the start (left or right) and slowly fade the intermediate rewards. Your goal is to have your dog do two full figure eights before getting a reward.

INTRODUCE CLOSE

Once your dog is successfully following your hand, you can begin training close. Use treats for these exercises and remember to work both the left and right sides.

1. With dog in a wait on your right side, move one arm's length forward. Keep your stance open. Your left foot should be a short step ahead of your right foot. Keep your arm extended at hip height or lower toward the dog, with treat between fingers. Look directly back at the dog. Your shoulder should be relaxed and down so your eyes can look down your arm at your dog.

Trouble Shooting: If your dog moves before you give the release command, gently reposition in the exact spot. Try again. If the dog continues to break, stop working on close and go back and review the wait exercises, particularly those where you face away from the dog.

2. Release and lure the dog forward with the treat to your right leg. When your dog begins to move, step forward on the right. Keep moving forward as you draw the dog's nose to the back of your leg. Your pinkie finger should be touching the *back* of your leg. Click when your dog's nose reaches your hand. Reward with treat.

Trouble Shooting: If your dog does not follow your hand, use a larger, smellier treat and make sure the dog knows the treat is in your hand. This is a follow-the-hand drill, so do not use a toy.

Trouble Shooting: If your dog passes your leg or shifts his rear end away from you, shorten the distance between you and the dog (e.g., put your hand on his nose). You can also do this drill next to a wall or fence. With the dog between you and the wall, he cannot mooch forward. With each successful close, move one dog width farther from the wall.

With success, slowly (in one-foot increments) increase the distance to four feet then six feet and then twelve feet. As the distance between you lengthens, keep your dog focused on you. Do not let him scan the surroundings, sniff the ground, or scratch an ear while you are moving into position. Remember his wait should be active, which means his focus remains on you and he is ready to move.

As you do multiple reps to increase the distance, you should add a verbal command. We use *Close* and we use it on both the left and right sides. For dogs that are obedience trained, you can use *Close* on the left and select another word for the right, such as *Side* or *In*.

In the introduction, you positioned your dog directly behind you and worked the simplest close—a straight line. However, your dog must be able to find close from a variety of positions. Close is an integral part of agility course work, and you should work these drills continuously. A touch of groundwork training can clarify your team's communication paths, particularly when you begin short sequence work. These drills also work very well during warm-ups.

Close position is arm and hip back, drawing dog behind handler.

Close work also provides an excellent opportunity to proof your dog's wait and release. Remember to reward the wait frequently and use a consistent, clear release word.

AROUND THE CLOCK

With success on a straight line close, you should begin to introduce angles. Picture a clock. Your dog is at twelve o'clock, and you are standing in the middle. Call your dog to *Close* on the right side and move forward toward six o'clock. This is the basic or straight line close that you taught in the introduction. Once the dog is doing a straight, consistent close, we immediately introduce angles.

For this exercise you stand in the center of the "clock." Keep an open stance (left foot in front of right or vice versa). Keep your arm extended toward the dog and keep your eyes on him. As your dog begins to move, arc your arm around into the close position to help draw the dog behind you.

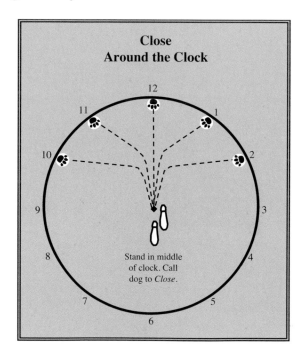

1. Place your dog at the one o'clock position. The working distance for close drills is twelve to fifteen feet. This gives your dog enough room to arc into position.

2. Move to the center of the "clock" and face the direction you will be moving. Connect with your dog. Release by saying "Okay. Close," and immediately move forward toward six o'clock.

Trouble Shooting **If your dog slices directly to you, he will end up ahead of your position. Try again and guide him sideways in a small arc with your extended arm before dropping your hand to the close position.**

3. Mark the final position (i.e., dog slightly behind your leg and spine parallel to your body position) and reward in position.

Repeat with the dog at the two, eleven, and then ten o'clock positions. Notice how far sideways your dog must travel from the two and ten o'clock positions before coming up behind you into close. Remember to work both the left and right sides.

AROUND A WING

Once your dog is successfully finding close from a variety of angles, you can begin to work around an obstacle. Use a wing stanchion, a short piece of fence, or a set of chairs. There are three positions for the dog and three positions for the handler.

Do not move to the next position until your dog is consistently successful. Keep an open stance (left foot in front of right or vice versa). Keep your arm extended toward the dog and keep your eyes on him. As your dog begins to move, arc your arm behind your body and then into the close position.

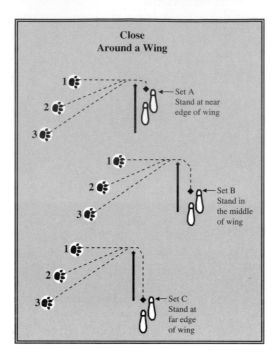

Close Around a Wing

Set A
Stand at near edge of wing

Set B
Stand in the middle of wing

Set C
Stand at far edge of wing

1. Place the dog at a distance of about fifteen feet at position 1, which is even with one side of the wing.

2. Stand even or parallel to the dog but on the opposite side of the wing. Face the direction you will be moving.

3. Connect with your dog. Release by saying "Okay. Close." When your dog comes around the corner of the wing, move forward. Keep the dog between you and the wing.

Trouble Shooting: If your dog comes to your front, reduce the distance from the wing and work in smaller increments. Exaggerate your arm movement in an arc before dropping your hand to close. This is a common mistake with obedience trained dogs.

4. Mark and reward in close position.

Complete Set A with the dog at positions 2 and 3. Work both the left and right sides. Then repeat the whole sequence (positions 1, 2, 3) from the middle of the wing, which is Set B. In this set you are standing parallel to your dog when he is at position 2. And finally, repeat the sequence (positions 1, 2, 3) from the far edge of the wing, which is Set C. In this set you are standing parallel to the dog when he is at position 3.

FIRST STEP

As you begin to work angles and around obstacles, be very clear as to which direction your first step goes. The first step is critical. This is the piece of information your dog uses to determine his direction. If you are facing left and take that first step left, your dog will move to the left first. He may redirect with you on your second, third, or fourth steps, but his first and primary direction will be to the left. Your first step is vital. It is the primary directional for your dog, particularly when you are reconnecting. As a team you must reconnect after every lead-out, contact, tunnel, and handling move, such as a front or rear cross. In all of these, in every sequence, the direction of your first step will be your dog's biggest clue to where he should move.

U-TURN

The U-turn—either to the left or right—is an excellent exercise to ensure that the dog is following the handler's hand. It also teaches the dog to chase the hand. Since your turn—being on the inside of the U-turn—is shorter, your dog must travel farther to keep up with the treat hand. Start with motion and a visible treat. Work both the left and right sides.

1. With the dog moving at your left side, turn gently to the right into a loopy U-turn. Keep the treat on your dog's nose for the first few turns. Encourage him to increase his pace with a bit of verbal praise. Move through the turn and straight ahead on the way out.

2. After a few U-turns, keep the treat a few inches ahead of your dog's nose as you turn. Keep your hand at your side (right along your pant seam). Try the following:

- Tighten the U-turn. Instead of a loopy curve, make it a true U shape.

- Increase your pace. Be sure your dog is chasing your hand.

- Do multiple U-turns in quick succession

As you work to tighten the U-turn and focus your dog's attention on your hands, you are also teaching him to watch your motion. A turn is signaled by a shoulder/hip turn. Keep your body language clear; let your feet, hips, and shoulders flow through the turn, particularly when you begin to tighten the turn. Do not do the turn in one step. At this stage a clear turn signal requires two or three steps.

SIDE SPIN

The side spin—left or right—is another wonderful exercise to ensure that the dog is following the handler's hand. It also teaches the dog to move its rear around without traveling forward and is a prerequisite to teaching the *Back* command. This is not a trick. Make sure your dog follows your hand through the spin, not just spins in place, and be sure to work on both the left and right sides. Your dog should be able to circle almost any obstacle, such as a plastic cone, jump stanchion, trash can, or stool. Start slowly with a visible treat.

1. With the dog moving at your left side, lure his nose a few inches (about the length of your dog's head) forward—ahead of your leg.

2. Turn your hand away from your body and draw a full curve back to your leg. Let your dog's nose, head, and body follow your hand around the circle. Keep moving forward. Your dog should have to chase you for a step or two to catch up.

Add a verbal command, like *Spin, Flip,* or *Around.*

FRONT CROSS

Once your dog is reliably following your hand, you can begin adding in simple front crosses. In agility a front cross is defined as a point on the course where the handler crosses in front or ahead of the dog's path. In most front crosses, the handler—for a brief moment—is facing the dog. As the handler crosses the dog's path, the dog switches from the handler's right hand to the left (or vice versa). Similar to the figure eight exercise, the goal with front crosses on the flat is to get your dog focused on the hand switch. There are two front cross exercises.

Straight Line Front Cross

The simplest front cross is executed on a straight line. Use a wall, section of driveway, or sidewalk to ensure that you are moving straight into and out of the drill. Remember to work both sides and keep moving.

1. Put your dog in a wait about ten feet away.

2. Face the direction (forward) you will be moving with your arm extended toward the dog. Hold a visible, easy-to-handle treat in the extended hand. Release the dog by saying "Okay. Close." To your dog this looks like a simple, straight line close.

3. As your dog begins moving toward you, rotate toward the dog (step back rather than forward) and switch the treat from hand to hand. For one brief moment you are facing the dog. Keep your arms extended toward your dog as you make the exchange. Move forward immediately with your arm extended toward the dog on the "new" side.

4. Mark the final close position on the new side. Reward.

Turning Front Cross

The second front cross combines a side change with a direction change. In this exercise as your dog approaches the close position, you turn toward the dog and step off at a ninety degree angle. For example, if the dog comes to a left-side close, step back and then to the right. Thus the dog finishes on your right side and is perpendicular to where he started.

1. Put your dog in a wait about ten feet away.

2. Face forward with your arm extended toward the dog. Hold a visible, easy-to-handle treat in the extended hand. Release the dog by saying "Okay. Close."

3. As your dog approaches your finger tips, step back (feet together) and switch the treat from hand to hand. For one brief moment you are facing the dog before you rotate to the new direction. Keep your arm extended toward your dog as you make the exchange.

4. Step forward immediately with your dog following the treat in the new hand. You completed a 270 degree turn, and your dog did a ninety degree turn. Mark the final close position on the new side. Reward.

Back

The *Back* command turns the dog away from the handler. It also allows the handler to switch the dog from side-to side. In its simplest form, a back is half of a side spin. It can also be thought of as side-by-side U-turns. The objective is to get the dog to move slightly ahead of the handler, turn away, and then return to the close position on the handler's opposite side. This drill also reinforces attention to hand signals and is the foundation for a rear cross. In agility a rear cross is defined as a point on the course where the handler crosses behind the dog's path. As the handler crosses behind the dog, the dog switches from the handler's right hand to the left (or vice versa).

In a rear cross, the handler moves across the dog's path as the dog moves ahead.
(Photo courtesy of Joe Canova)

INTRODUCE BACK

1. Put treats in both hands.

2. With the dog moving into close, lure the dog's nose forward with a treat in the right hand (like the beginning of a side spin). The dog's head must be ahead of your leg.

3. Turn your hand away from your body (same as a side spin), but as the dog turns to the right, you also turn to the right—do not travel sideways through the turn. Stand up and pivot.

Trouble Shooting: If your dog halts rather than turns, use more forward motion and let your dog move farther ahead of your leg before turning his nose away from you. Remember: Your dog's nose is following your hand. It is your hand's motion forward that puts the dog in position.

4. Move forward immediately after turning and call dog to close on the left. Reward with treat in left hand.

Trouble Shooting: If your dog hesitates through the turn, goose him (playfully) in the rear end or gently swing his rear end around as you pass behind him. A little guidance in the middle of the turn can reassure your dog that he is supposed to turn away.

With multiple reps switch right-to-left and then left-to-right. This is where you should add a verbal command. We typically use *Back*. Some of our students who do obedience and rally use *Flip* or *Turn* to prevent confusion with *Get Back*.

Training Tip

If you have trouble picturing the flow of the *Back* command, place a cone or stool on the floor six feet in front of you. With dog in close, move forward to the stool and swing your dog all the way around the stool. This is a side spin around an obstacle. Do not circle the stool yourself. Stay on the approach side. When your dog returns to you, move forward away from the stool. To turn the side spin into a back, return to your original point and go forward again. Swing your dog around the stool, but when the dog is opposite you, turn toward the dog and then walk back in the direction you came.

For back, lure dog's nose ahead of body and turn his nose away from your leg.

PRACTICE DRILLS

You now have enough groundwork commands (*Close, U-Turn, Spin, Back*) to begin working short sequences. The following are some simple examples. Be creative! And work from a walk to a crisp walk to a trot to a run. As your speed increases, be careful to keep your hand signals clear. Do not rush the hand signal. If you look like you are swatting flies, your dog will not move with you!

- Call dog to *Close*, execute a U-turn, a straight line front cross, and then ask for a *Back*. As your dog begins to turn, complete your turn quickly and move forward briskly. Let your dog chase you into close position after each turn or side switch.

- Do two close-back drills in a row. Thus your dog goes from the right side to the left and then back again. Chain together two, three, four, or even five in a row.

- Speed up and run between backs. Let your dog chase you into close and increase the distance between backs to twenty or thirty feet.

As you work these drills, if your dog lags, reward him immediately for catching up to your hand. If your dog passes you, stop and repeat the close drills. The intent of groundwork is to get your dog to follow your hand motions. If your hand does not move five feet ahead of your body, why did your dog go there?

Out

All the previous exercises worked the dog at the handler's side—right or left. In agility the dog is often required to work at a distance, either ahead, behind, or to the side of the handler. Even on straight lines the handler and dog may take slightly different paths. When the dog works at a distance directly to the left or right of the handler's side—five, ten, or even twenty feet away—this is called lateral distance.

Teaching a dog to work at a distance is a process. So far the dog has been rewarded for following or moving with the handler's motion. He has also been rewarded for staying close to the handler. The out exercise separates two of the primary signal methods or directionals. A directional is a piece of information your dog uses to determine where you are going and where he should go. In agility there are four directionals: motion, the direction you are facing, a hand signal, and a verbal command. By far the strongest directional is motion. Your dog's basic pack instinct will tell him to move with you. The second-strongest directional is where you are looking or facing. The third-strongest directional is your hand signal, and the weakest directional is a verbal command. Particularly with dogs that bark incessantly on course, a verbal command can be almost useless.

In all the previous groundwork drills, we deliberately kept the directionals balanced. You moved where you were looking and directed the dog with a hand and verbal signal that supported your motion. With out, the dog follows the handler's motion but must interpret the extended arm as a direction to move away or maintain a lateral distance. The verbal command for lateral distance is *Out*. Since we are asking the dog to ignore the primary directional (motion), we teach the out in very short increments. It is also vital to preserve the dog's instinct to follow the primary directional (aka motion) so we also do lots of close drills while working out.

INTRODUCE OUT

1. Place a trash can or wing-jump stanchion on a thirty degree angle about ten feet away.

2. With your dog in a right-side close, move forward directly at the wing or can. When you are a few feet away from the obstacle, extend your arm, luring the dog's nose away from your body. Extend your arm around or over the obstacle, drawing the dog around the opposite side. Keep moving for-

ward past the obstacle. Thus you and the dog passed the obstacle together but on opposite sides.

3. Complete by returning the dog to a right-side close. Keep moving until your dog catches you.

Repeat multiple times and then add a verbal command. This should be *Out* or *Away.* Make sure your arm is fully extended when you give the verbal command. Switch sides and repeat the exercise on the left.

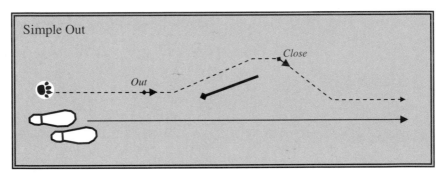

Simple Out
Close
Out

Be careful to keep your arm and hand low. A hand signal above your head is too high for most dogs to see, much less follow, and is also hard to maintain as a signal when you begin to move faster. Keep your voice calm. Do not shout. Even at ten or twenty feet, your dog can hear you. It is not necessary to increase the volume of your commands. An overly loud command is more likely to draw your dog back to you. And be careful to reward your dog for moving away. Verbally mark his motion away. If you skip the mark, you are simply rewarding him for returning to close. This will diminish his interest in out.

Signal *Out* with an extended arm.

PRACTICE DRILLS

Lateral distance is important but must be trained in balance with all the close work. We work all the dogs—regardless of size and breed—on the same out drills.

- Over the next four or five repetitions, change the angle of the wing until it is perpendicular to your path. Continue to give a *Close* command before and after each *Out* command.

- Slowly—in one-foot increments—move your path away from the wing. Continue walking on a parallel path to your dog and make sure your arm is fully extended toward your dog to encourage him to stay on his own path.

- Begin moving faster, but remember your forward motion will act as a magnet, drawing your dog in. Get your dog moving away before you increase your forward speed. Keep your arm extended.

Groundwork Sequences

With *Close*, *Back*, and *Out* commands, you can run your dog through some complicated groundwork sequences. Combining groundwork commands into short sequences allows you to proof the verbal commands and hand signals with motion. This is where the dog and handler learn to move and flow together.

SINGLE WAVE

With four wing-jump stanchions, chairs, or trash cans set fifteen feet apart, weave dog in and out using alternating *Out* and *Close* commands. Begin at a walk and exaggerate your hand signals on the first couple of passes. If your dog forges ahead, slow your pace and bring your dog all the way to close before moving forward into an out. Complete the exercises with you dog on left and right. With four obstacles you can do two easy sequences:

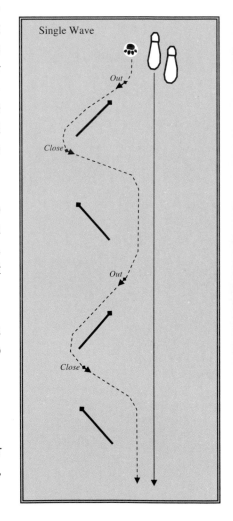

Single Wave

- Start with a moving close, do an out, then a close, then an out. End with a running close. Remember to do both the left and right sides.

- Start with out, do a close, an out, and then a close. Refer to diagram.

DOUBLE WAVE

With four wing-jump stanchions or four trash cans set fifteen feet apart, weave dog in and out using *Out* and *Close* commands. At the fourth stanchion, do a U-turn or a back to turn dog and weave back up the line. Do multiple repetitions and increase your speed with each try. With four obstacles, you can do a variety of short sequences.

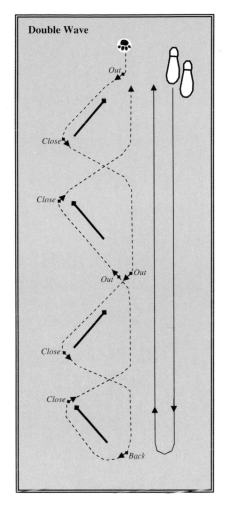

Double Wave

- Start with a close, out, close sequence. With the last *Out* command, do a side switch to close on the opposite side. Weave back to start using, out, close, out.

- Start with out, close, out. After the last *Close* command, give an immediate *Back* command (luring dog around last wing) and then on the return do close, out, close. Refer to diagram.

As your speed increases, pay attention to when you give the hand signal and verbal command. When you go faster, your partner needs information sooner.

LONG OUT

With two wing-jump stanchions or two trash cans set twenty-five feet apart, begin increasing the distance of your dog's out. Stand between the two wings and send your dog *out* around the first wing, stepping forward in the direction you want the dog to go. As your dog passes around the obstacle, step back and call to *Close*. Reward and immediately send into second out. With each repetition, slowly tighten your own circle by reducing your steps forward. Your body, hand and arm, however, continue to signal out. With each repetition, you remain closer to the center of the two obstacles and your dog increases the distance he travels away from you.

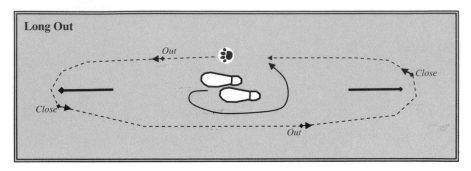

OUT TO BACK

Another variation with two wing stanchions or trash cans is to combine out and back. These drills allow the handler to change hands by crossing behind the dog or keep the dog on the same side by crossing behind and then crossing in front. These exercises are excellent warm-ups for advanced handling work. Try experimenting with different combinations, such as out-close-back or out-close-out. You can also try a full figure 8, which is out-close-back-close.

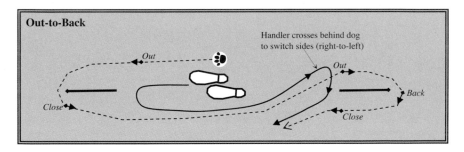

WING BOX

With four wing-jump stanchions or trash cans, combine the out, back, and wave drills to work hand and verbal commands. There are a wide variety of combinations possible. Remember to work both the left and right sides.

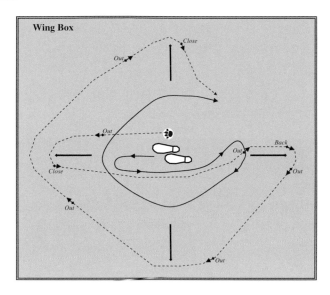

Go On

Another important groundwork skill is the *Go* or *Go On* command. This simple command allows the dog to pass the handler to complete the obstacle or obstacles ahead. As a groundwork skill, go is taught as an

extension of target training. This makes it a fun game for handler and dog. In this drill it is important to keep moving forward. The dog is not learning to ignore the handler's motion. He is learning to move ahead of the handler's motion. This is a critical distinction and is important for sequencing and contact work.

A *Go On* sends the dog ahead of the handler through the tire.

INTRODUCE GO ON

1. With a visible target about twenty-five feet away, move forward with the dog in close.

2. Halfway to the target (about twelve feet back), send the dog ahead to the target. Use a forward hand signal and look at the target. Walk in slowly behind dog.

Trouble Shooting: If your dog stops and comes back, walk with the dog to the target and show your dog a treat on the target. Move forward with the dog to within six feet of the target before sending ahead. Gradually work backward, sending the dog ahead for longer distances with each repetition.

Repeat on the opposite side and add a verbal command, like *Go* or *Go On*.

CHAPTER 7

Tunnels

An all-round dog favorite and one of the easiest obstacles to train is the tunnel. From terriers to Border collies, a tunnel entices and intrigues most dogs. For agility trainers the tunnel provides the perfect obstacle to reinforce and proof all your groundwork training.

Equipment Description

Although the United Kennel Club (UKC) has four different tunnel styles, most agility organizations have two types of tunnels: an open tunnel and a closed tunnel.

OPEN TUNNEL

An open or pipe tunnel is a flexible tube with two open ends. Both ends should be about twenty-four inches in diameter, although Teacup Agility prefers a sixteen-inch diameter tunnel. Across registries, tunnels range in length from eight to twenty feet. Every tunnel must be secured at both ends to prevent movement while the dog is running through, and longer tunnels must also be secured in the middle. Most registries require that competition tunnels be opaque (not seethrough) but not black. Tunnels are available in dozens of different colors including white, pink, red, yellow, green, blue, and purple.

On an agility course open tunnels are laid straight, gently curved, or twisted into a variety of shapes. The most common are C and L shapes, but some registries allow an S shape. Tunnels can be between jumps, wrapped under the A-frame or dog walk, or curved around a pause table. There can be one, two, or three tunnels on typical AKC or

USDAA courses, and one of the NADAC games classes, Tunnelers, is an entire course of tunnels.

CLOSED TUNNEL

A closed or collapsed tunnel—also known as a chute—consists of a rigid entrance section with a flexible fabric chute attached. The dog must enter the rigid section and then push through the collapsed cloth to the end. The rigid section, which is two to three feet in length and twenty-four inches in diameter, is usually a heavy-duty plastic barrel, a wood or metal doghouse, or a short pipe tunnel. The attached chute is generally constructed of a lightweight, water-resistant fabric such as ripstop nylon or pack cloth. The length of the chute ranges from eight to twelve feet. It is attached to the barrel and flares slightly at the end.

OTHER TUNNELS

The UKC agility program allows for two other types of tunnels. The crawl tunnel is a rectangular-shaped tunnel that consists of fabric stretched over a PVC-pipe frame. The overall dimensions of the obstacle

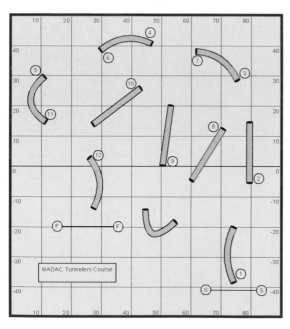

are approximately thirty inches wide and six feet long with adjustable heights of eight, twelve, sixteen, twenty, and twenty-four inches. The hoop tunnel consists of hoops, constructed of flexible three-quarter-inch piping or plastic hula hoops, held in place on a PVC-pipe or wood frame. A total of eight hoops are attached and set at alternating angles of approximately sixty degrees to one another, forming a zigzag pattern when viewed from above.

Training–Open Tunnels

Dogs and kids love tunnels. Tunnels are fun to crawl through, hide in, and play around. Many puppy kindergarten classes use soft nylon children's tunnels during puppy playtime. Tunnel introduction is a simple process and is the same for all dogs regardless of size and age. It is also a shaped behavior and, as such, must be offered. Never push, force, or pull a reluctant or cautious dog through a tunnel.

Driving out of a tunnel.

Certain breeds—like terriers—take to tunnel training like ducks to water. It is instinctive. Many dogs see a wide-open tunnel and blast through it. If you own one of these dogs, then tunnel training becomes anti-tunnel training. You may spend hours teaching your dog that she cannot take the tunnel *unless told to do so*. If your dog is already running through the tunnel, you can skip the tunnel introduction exercise.

INTRODUCE THE TUNNEL

The simplest method to begin tunnel training requires the help of a trainer or friend who holds the dog. Use a twenty-four-inch-diameter tunnel that is shrunk to about three feet in length. Soft bag tunnel holders filled with sand are fine, but remove any metal bases that can clank or rattle. If you remove the tunnel holders, put the tunnel against a wall to keep it steady. Most tunnels are heavy enough to stay put, but you want to ensure that the tunnel does not roll during the introduction phase. At Mountain Freaks the entire tunnel introduction generally takes about fifteen minutes. We then repeat the process—from beginning to end—for the next two training sessions.

1. Have the dog holder sit on the floor with the dog and let the dog sniff and investigate the tunnel. Hold dog gently by his collar, but do not force him forward.

> **Trouble Shooting:** If your dog balks at the mere sight of the tunnel, move back five or six feet and sit quietly with him. Let a dog that likes the tunnel run through it. Throw a toy through the tunnel and let the second dog chase the toy through the tunnel. Dogs can learn by watching. Some dogs do not understand what you want when faced with a scrunched up tunnel. It looks strange and smells odd. Letting them watch another dog is a simple way to get the idea across.

2. Go to the opposite end of the tunnel, kneel down, and look at your dog through the tunnel. Extend your hand through the tunnel with a toy or treat. Call the dog softly. Your dog holder must keep him from going around or over the tunnel to you, which is a common response when you call the dog.

3. Extend a favorite treat or toy through the tunnel and lure the dog forward. Mark and reward for any motion forward into the tunnel (nose, paw touch, or body lean), but remember to "up the ante" after each success. Offer a jackpot for his first pass through the tunnel. Your trainer/friend holding

the dog should remain neutral, simply preventing the dog from going around the tunnel. Repeat multiple times and try tunnels of different colors, if they are available.

> **Trouble Shooting:** If your dog balks at entering the tunnel, but does not seem afraid of it, you can let him chase another dog through the tunnel. Line them up—nose to tail—with the friendly, tunnel savvy dog in front. Hold your dog in a restrained send and let go as the first dog enters the tunnel. Make this a game and do not force the tunnel entry.

> **Trouble Shooting:** If the dog is not willing to step into the tunnel, extend your hand farther into the tunnel or wiggle an enticing toy in the middle. Do not climb into the tunnel yourself. Your motion into and backing out of the tunnel will cause it to rock and move. Worried dogs find this more confusing and frightening. Squish the tunnel up tighter or use a thin, nylon tunnel.

Repeat the shaping exercise multiple times. Mark and reward only when the dog's entire body is inside the tunnel. Novice dogs frequently stick their heads and necks into the tunnel, at which point the holder lets go, but then the dog backs out. Your dog holder should not grab at the dog. Let the dog make a mistake and simply try again.

Once your dog is moving through the tunnel, have the dog holder use a restrained send to increase the drive and speed through the tunnel. Stay visible, but gradually move away from the end of the tunnel. Shift backward in one-foot increments to about ten feet. Once your dog is pulling at the tunnel entrance and moving briskly through, hold your own dog in a restrained send. Return to the tunnel entrance and hold the dog very close to the tunnel (nose almost inside). Release and move forward with the dog. Meet your dog at the opposite end with a reward.

If your dog refuses to go through the tunnel without you at the opposite end, go back a step. To wean the dog off the holder and the lure, have your trainer/friend hold the dog again and call the dog from different positions.

- Let the dog see you through the tunnel, but do not lure with treat.

- Stand up so the dog can see only your legs.

- Stand to the side of the tunnel.

TRAIN THE TUNNEL

Tunnels are deceptive. The idea is simple, but the actual execution and training are a tad more complex. The first step after the introduction is to get the dog to work a long straight tunnel, and the second step is to add the verbal command.

Use a restrained send and place a target or toy three dog lengths from the end of the tunnel. Lengthen the tunnel slowly in two- or three-foot increments. Vary the color of the tunnel, if possible.

- Lengthen from three feet to five feet

- Lengthen from five feet to eight feet

- Lengthen from eight feet to twelve feet

- Full length

The next step is to add a verbal command. Common choices are *Tunnel*, *Chute*, or *Thru*. Hold your dog right at the end of the tunnel (one dog length). Give the verbal command and then release the dog to and through the tunnel and move forward with him. Mark as the dog's entire body disappears inside the tunnel. Reward with a toy or treat tossed a foot or two in front of the tunnel.

- Back up two dog lengths from the tunnel, give verbal command, and release

- Back up three dog lengths from the tunnel, give verbal command, and release

- Back up five dog lengths from the tunnel, give verbal command, and release

Move back only after two successes. If the dog does not go into the tunnel when released, do not try to fix the send. Gently retrieve the dog and move him closer (half the distance of the previous try) and resend. Your goal with this drill sequence is to get your dog to drive to the tunnel on the verbal command.

When teaching a verbal command, be careful to use just that one word. Do not preface your *Tunnel* command with extra words like "Ready! Ready!," another command such as *Go* or *Go On,* or the dog's name. Remember: If you call your dog's name, he should look at you. During obstacle training you want him to look at the obstacle, not you.

TEACH ANGLE ENTRIES

Once your dog is driving forward through a straight tunnel, you can then further your dog's understanding of how to execute a tunnel by teaching angle entries and by using different tunnel shapes. Your dog should be able to find the tunnel entrance from straight on, from an angle (forty-five degrees), and from the side of the tunnel. All of these tunnel entrances appear different to your dog.

Sit on the floor at dog height. If you sit directly in front of a straight tunnel, you can see through to the end. There is literally a light at the end of the tunnel. If you sit at an angle (try thirty degrees), you see the wall of the tunnel. This is what disorients dogs, even those that know the tunnel. Where's the hole? How do you get in? If you sit facing the side of a straight tunnel, it is even worse. From the side (or laterally), your dog cannot see even a partial entry. Over the course of several months, your tunnel training needs to expose your dog to all these variations.

The following exercise uses a restrained send to a tossed toy or treat. Move forward as you release the dog but watch him to be sure he is committed to the tunnel. Mark only after the dog's entire body is inside the tunnel. Use the following around-the-clock progression to train angle entries:

- Back up three dog lengths from the tunnel and align your dog with the tunnel entry (straight on or twelve o'clock position), give a verbal command, release, mark, and then reward forward as your dog exits the tunnel.

- Back up four dog lengths from the tunnel and two dog lengths to the left side (thirty degree angle or one o'clock), give a verbal command, release, mark, and then reward forward as your dog exits the tunnel.

- Back up six dog lengths from the tunnel and four dog lengths to the left side (sixty degree angle or two o'clock), give a verbal command, release, mark, and then reward forward as your dog exits the tunnel.

- Back up eight dog lengths from the tunnel and six dog lengths to the left side (just short of ninety degrees or three o'clock), give a verbal command, release, mark, and then reward forward as your dog exits the tunnel.

- Repeat this sequence on the right side.

Should your dog miss the tunnel entry or turn back to you, remember the two strikes rule. After every mistake, retry once and then simplify the exercise. The above sequence should be done over the course of several training sessions, not a few hours. Keep increasing the distance from the tunnel in addition to the angle.

EXPLORE TUNNEL SHAPES

Tunnels, particularly a twenty- or twenty-four-foot tunnel, can be sculpted into multiple shapes. The most common are L, S, and C shapes. With each bend, light is reduced and the interior of the tunnel is darker. Dogs must also reduce speed to navigate the turns, although many nimble canines learn to bank around the sides of the tunnel—NASCAR-style.

Introduce curved tunnels slowly to keep your dog's confidence and interest high. All of the following exercises use a restrained send to a thrown treat or toy. Mark once the dog's entire body is inside the tunnel. Toss the reward in front of the tunnel. Work through the following shapes:

- L tunnel with the short end of the L as the exit point

- C tunnel with a flat curve; start with a skinny (and progresses to a plump C

- L tunnel with the short end of the L as the entry point

- S tunnel

- U tunnel

Tunnels are often wrapped under the dog walk or A-frame.

On course, tunnels are also placed around the pause table, under the A-frame, or wrapped around the dog walk. Each configuration looks different to your dog, so be patient and rework the tunnel send drills as needed.

TEACH A CONNECTED EXIT

Once the dog is executing a variety of tunnel shapes at different angles, it is time to put you—the handler—into the game. In addition to working close, this drill also gives you a chance to practice your timing. Call your dog while he is still in the tunnel. Do not wait until your dog has exited to let him know where you are and what you want next—connect as he exits. Watch the ribs of the tunnel. For medium- and large-weight dogs, the ribs wiggle as the dog goes through, giving you an indication of where the dog is. Use a skinny (-shaped) tunnel for these drills.

1. Set up dog about twenty feet from the tunnel entrance. Stand five or six feet in front of dog (i.e., between dog and tunnel).

2. Release dog to tunnel and move immediately to the tunnel exit. If your dog is really fast in the tunnel, you may need a longer lead out. Call your dog as he passes the mid-point of the tunnel.

3. Call your dog to *Close* as he exits the tunnel. Keep moving forward. Reward when dog reaches your side.

Side Switch: Entrance

With an L-shaped tunnel, send the dog to the long side of the tunnel from eight to ten feet away. Once the dog is committed and has entered the tunnel, switch sides before passing the tunnel entry. Thus you are calling your dog to *Close* on the opposite side as he exits the short end of the tunnel. For example, if your dog went into the tunnel on your left, he should complete the exercise on your right. You crossed behind the dog's path to execute the side switch.

Side Switch: End

With a C-shaped tunnel, send dog to the tunnel from eight to ten feet away. Once dog is committed and has entered the tunnel, switch to the opposite side of the tunnel. Call your dog to *Close* on the new side. For example, if your dog went into the tunnel on your left, he should complete the exercise with a right-side close. You should turn into (momentarily face) the tunnel as you cross past the exit. This is considered a front-cross; you crossed ahead of the dog's path.

Tunnel vs Wait

Another excellent groundwork drill is to put the dog in a wait near the tunnel entrance. Start fifteen or twenty feet away and rework the wait drills (i.e., walk in front, bend down to tie shoe, walk a circle around him). Reward the wait frequently and before he breaks. With success move your dog closer to the tunnel in five-foot increments.

Tunnel vs Close

Another excellent drill with a C-shaped tunnel is to walk your dog in close position back and forth in front of or parallel to the two tunnel entrances. Every fourth or fifth pass, send your dog to one of the tunnel entrances. Immediately call your dog back to *Close* and resume moving past the tunnel entrances. Use *Close* and *Back* commands to vary your dog's path and keep his attention on your hand. Start ten or fifteen feet away from the tunnel and with success move closer to the tunnel in two-foot increments. Reward the close. This drill is critical for dogs that love the tunnel. Your dog should not take the tunnel unless you give him a verbal command to do so.

Go Tunnel!

Set up a tunnel game. Can your dog reliably find a tunnel entrance from fifteen feet? How about twenty feet? How about forty feet? Start close and move backward in five-foot increments. Remember to use one verbal command and move forward after your dog is driving toward the tunnel. Do the game first with a straight tunnel and then move sideways and try an angled entry.

Find the Tunnel Entrance

Proof your dog's understanding of the tunnel by standing in the middle of a straight, twelve- or fifteen-foot tunnel. Face one end of the tunnel. Send your dog with an arm signal and verbal command to the tunnel entrance, but do not move. Your dog should be able to loop away from you and find the entrance on his own. If your dog does not immediately find the entrance, move a few feet closer to the entrance and try again.

Training—Closed Tunnel

The closed tunnel or chute is actually quite a bit different from an open tunnel. Although it is generally introduced and taught at the same time as the pipe tunnel, dogs must learn a different skill set for the chute. Chutes also vary in construction more than tunnels do. Barrels come in a bewildering variety of shapes, heights, and sizes. In most registries the minimum height is twenty-four inches, but often the barrel is higher or not a barrel at all. It is not uncommon to find a barrel shaped like a doghouse. Another consideration is the type of fabric and length of the chute, which can vary from eight to twelve feet.

Zoie zips out of the chute heading for her handler. (Photo courtesy of Joe Canova)

Weather is also a major issue when working a chute outdoors. Lightweight fabrics can blow open on their own, making the closed chute a wonderful straight tunnel. While fun for the dog, the handler can be left flatfooted as the dog races ahead. On the other hand, the chute can twist in the wind, necessitating extra weights or tie-downs of the chute ends, making it more difficult for the dog to push through. And a soaking rain can make a chute nearly impossible to push open, particularly for little dogs. Dogs with thin coats also find the wet fabric uncomfortable as it slides across their back. Some registries allow the ring crew to hold a soaked chute open. While this helps the dog execute the obstacle, it also disturbs or startles some dogs to find a human standing next to them when they exit the chute.

As to the actual execution of the chute, the dog must learn to go straight and find his handler after exiting. A curved path toward either side of the chute causes the chute to twist, making it harder for the dog to exit. High-drive dogs often try to bank the chute, the same way they do the tunnel, and end up sliding out sideways or getting hopelessly tangled. Also remember that once the chute is closed, the dog pushes through with his eyes closed. This mean he exits "blind." In order to find his handler, the dog must listen for the handler's voice while still in the chute. And, as he enters the chute, the dog must pay attention to the handler's position and line of motion. This provides the dog with more information and direction as he exits.

INTRODUCE THE CHUTE

The closed tunnel is taught in three phases: barrel, open chute, and closed chute. Unlike the tunnel introduction, the chute introduction should be spread over many training sessions, and the open tunnel should be introduced first. Chute training requires the help of a trainer or friend who holds the dog in the first phase and the chute open in the second phase. Anchor the barrel to ensure that it does not rock or slide during the introduction phase.

1. Roll up the chute or remove it so you can introduce the dog to the barrel first. Sit on the floor with your dog, and let him

sniff and investigate the barrel. Hold the dog gently by the collar, but do not force him forward.

Trouble Shooting: If your dog balks at the mere sight of the barrel, move back five or six feet and sit quietly with him. Let a dog that likes the barrel run through it. Throw a toy through the barrel, and let the second dog chase the toy through the barrel. Dogs learn by watching. Some dogs do not understand what you want when faced with a scrunched up chute at the end of a plastic barrel. It looks strange, sounds weird, and smells odd. Letting them watch another dog is a simple way to get the idea across.

2. Have your friend/instructor hold the dog at one end of the barrel. Go to the opposite end, kneel down, and look at your dog through the barrel. Call softly to the dog. Mark and reward any head dip or focus through the barrel. Your dog holder must keep him from going around or over the barrel to you, which is a common response when you call the dog.

Trouble Shooting: If your dog does not like the feel of the barrel, let him enter through the scrunched up chute. A scrunched chute looks and feels like a tunnel, and some dogs accept this direction better. For the first two phases of the introduction, it does not matter which end the dog enters. Let your dog play!

3. Shape the barrel execution. The friend/instructor holding your dog should remain neutral, simply preventing the dog from going around the barrel. Extend a favorite treat or toy through the barrel and lure the dog forward. Mark and reward for any motion forward into the barrel (nose, paw touch, or body lean), but remember to "up the ante" after each success. Repeat multiple times and try different types of barrels, if they are available.

Once your dog is moving briskly through the barrel, hold him in a restrained send very close to the barrel (nose almost inside). Release and move forward with the dog. Meet your dog at the opposite end with a reward. If the dog refuses to go through the barrel without the handler being at the opposite end, wean the dog off the lure. Have your friend hold the dog again and call the dog from different positions. This is a simple progression, but do not move to the next step until the dog is successful.

- Let the dog see you through the barrel, but do not lure with a treat.

- Stand up so the dog can see only your legs.

- Stand to the side of the barrel.

The next step is to add the chute. Have your friend hold the scrunched up chute wide open but no longer than six feet in length. Every other time you send the dog through the barrel, extend the fabric chute two feet. Mark when the dog's entire body is inside the barrel. Novice dogs frequently stick their heads and necks into the barrel, but then back out. Continue extending the chute in two-foot increments until the dog is executing a full length, open chute that your friend is holding open.

The final stage is to close or drop the chute. Have your friend drop the fabric two or three inches after every successful pass through the chute. Mark when the dog's entire body is inside the chute. As the fabric gets close to the dog's back, allow the last foot of the chute to slide gently off the dog's back as he exits. Do not drop the chute on the dog until his nose and head are out. Once the dog is pushing through the last foot or so, hold open or arrange the chute to make a slight crease or ridge down the middle. This gives the dog a good idea of where to go, keeps him moving on a straight line thru the chute, and provides light inside the chute.

If you trained on a light-colored or lightweight chute, be sure to hold the chute open the first few times your dog encounters a dark-colored or heavy fabric chute. This is also true for chutes that are longer than those your dog trained on initially.

The next step is to add a verbal command. Common choices are *Chute* or *Thru*. Hold your dog right at the end of the chute (one dog length). Give the verbal command and then release dog to and through the chute. It is important to remain stationary. Mark as the dog's entire body disappears inside the barrel, and then move forward. As your dog exits the chute, throw a toy forward or drop a reward on the target.

TEACH ANGLE ENTRIES

Chute entries are different than tunnel entries. Dogs cannot bank the sides of a chute. If they do, they fall on their side and slide or get tangled. Dogs also need to learn to reconnect with their handler and/or find the next obstacle after exiting. Chute training also allows you to proof and refine your groundwork commands.

Your dog should be able to find the chute entrance from straight on, from an angle (forty-five degrees), and from the side. He must also learn to straighten out inside the barrel to ensure a straight line through the fabric portion. Do not switch sides on a chute until your dog has been working the chute successfully for several sessions. A side switch encourages your dog to angle through the chute, increasing the chance of a tangle.

The following exercises use a restrained send to a target or toy placed at the end of the chute, and you need a helper to hold the end of the chute open. Have your friend/instructor hold the end of the chute open, about six to eight inches off the floor. Mark once the dog's entire body is inside the chute, and move forward as you release your dog. Use the following around-the-clock progression to train angle entries:

- Back up three dog lengths from the chute and align your dog with the barrel entrance (straight on or twelve o'clock position), give a verbal command, release the dog, mark, and reward forward as the dog exits the chute.

- Back up four dog lengths from the tunnel and two dog lengths to the left side (thirty-degree angle or one o'clock), give a verbal command, release the dog, mark, and reward forward as the dog exits the chute.

- Back up six dog lengths from the tunnel and four dog lengths to the left side (sixty-degree angle or two o'clock), give a verbal command, release the dog, mark, and reward forward as the dog exits the chute.

- Back up eight dog lengths from the tunnel and six dog lengths to the left side (just short of ninety degrees or three o'clock), give a verbal command, release the dog, mark, and reward forward as the dog exits the chute.

Repeat this sequence on the right side and then repeat again—both left and right sides—with the chute closed. Should your dog miss the entrance or turn back to you, remember the two strikes rule. After every mistake, retry once and then simplify the exercise. The above sequence should be done over the course of weeks, not days or hours. Keep increasing the distance from the chute in addition to the angle.

TEACH CONNECTED EXIT

In addition to adding groundwork drills after the chute, this exercise gives the handler practice calling the dog while he is still in the chute. Do not wait until the dog has exited to let him know where you are and what you want next. It is important to connect as your dog exits the chute.

1. Set up the dog about twenty feet from the chute entrance. Stand five or six feet in front of the dog (i.e., between dog and chute).

2. Release the dog to the chute and move forward. Call your dog as he moves through the last third of the chute.

3. Call your dog to *Close* as he exits the chute. Keep moving forward. Reward when the dog reaches your side.

Chute vs Wait

Another excellent groundwork drill is to put dog in a wait in front of the chute. Work from twenty feet away and rework the wait drills (i.e., walk in front, bend down to tie shoe, walk a circle around him). With success, move your dog closer to the chute in five-foot increments.

Chute vs Close

Another excellent drill with a chute is to walk your dog in a close position back and forth in front of or parallel to the entrance. Every fourth or fifth pass, send your dog through the chute. Move to the end of the chute and immediately call your dog back to Close. Resume moving past the chute entrance. Use *Close* and *Back* commands to vary your path and keep your dog's attention on your hand. Start ten or fifteen feet away from the entrance, and with success move closer to the chute in short two-foot increments. This is an extremely important drill for dogs that love tunnels. Your dog must not take the chute until told to do so.

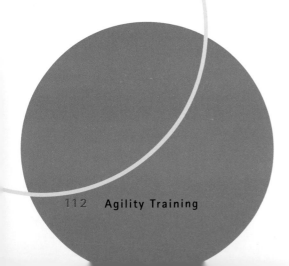

CHAPTER 8

Jumps

Agility is all about control and speed. It is also a jumping sport. Proportionally, there are many more jumps than any other type of equipment. A typical AKC or USDAA standard course with twenty obstacles has twelve to fourteen jumps. An AKC jumpers course is 90 percent jumps. A USDAA snookers course is typically 50 percent jumps. And almost every registry counts a dropped or knocked bar on a jump as an eliminating fault. Jumping agilely and efficiently is the most critical skill for an agility dog.

Equipment Description

Although the UKC has several unique jumps, most agility organizations have four main categories for jumps: bar, tire, panel, and spreads. Depending on the jump heights, every registry has slightly different requirements for their equipment. The following are general descriptions. If you are competition bound, then you should check the rules and regulations for the agility organization under which you want to trial.

HURDLES

A bar jump or hurdle is either one or two bars or PVC poles supported on either end. These are the most common jumps on an agility course. Across registries the typical height for the top bar is between eight and twenty-six inches. The most common jump heights are eight, twelve, sixteen, twenty, and twenty-four inches. With two bars the second bar is set at half the height of the top bar. Bar jumps are typically four or five feet wide. They can also have wings. A wing is an extension on the outside of the hurdle that extends the width of the obstacle, thereby forcing the dog and handler to work at a distance. Wings can be wood, plastic, or metal and can be a variety of shapes and sizes, including decorative flags, picket fence, PVC lattice, and cut-out animal shapes. Wing heights range upward from thirty-six inches and widths range from sixteen to thirty inches.

Ali's Border collie, Catcher, clears the first jump on a course with ease. (Photo courtesy of Joe Canova)

TIRE JUMP

Just as its name implies, a tire jump is a tire through which the dog jumps, although the "tire" is typically a section of flexible, four-inch plastic pipe shaped into a circle and covered in tape. A plastic tire is safer than a real tire, which is made of heavy rubber. Suspended in the center of a wood, metal, or PVC frame, the tire is hung at the same heights as a bar jump. The inside diameter of the tire is typically twenty-four inches, give or take an inch or two, although the USDAA program uses a seventeen- to twenty-inch diameter tire.

SPREAD JUMPS

For most registries there are three types of spread jumps: double, triple, and broad or long. The UKC also allows a water jump. Spread jumps are typically five feet wide.

Double Jump

The double jump is basically two hurdles spaced half the height of the jump apart. A double jump can be two single bar jumps set side by side, or it can be designed with one frame for both bars. Either way, the height and spacing of the bars are the same. For example, a twenty-inch high jump has two parallel bars set ten inches apart. In order for the dogs to distinguish this jump, some registries place two bars in an X beneath the two horizontal bars. This also gives the jump a more solid appearance. Dogs must jump both bars cleanly.

A Border collie flies through the tire jump.

(Photo courtesy of Joe Canova)

A Doberman over a double jump.

Triple Jump

The triple jump is a series of three ascending bars. The horizontal distance is one half the jump height, and the vertical distance between the bars is one-quarter the jump height. For example, the twenty-inch triple jump has bars set at ten, fifteen, and twenty inches with a ten-inch spread across the three bars. The dog must jump all three bars cleanly.

Broad Jump

Also known as the long jump, the broad jump has two configurations: ascending and hogbacked. The broad jump, which is also used in obedience, is a wide, low jump. The raised boards can be six to eight inches in width but are only three to eight inches high. The broad jump is typically spread to twice the dog's jump height. For example, a twenty-inch dog must leap over a forty-inch broad jump. When constructed of eight-inch-wide panels, a forty-inch broad jump has about one and a half inches between boards. The broad jump also has poles marking the four corners. Dogs must jump all the boards—two, three, or four depending on the width of the jump—and must pass between the corner markers.

PANEL JUMP

The panel jump uses up to seven displaceable panels to give the impression of a solid wall from bottom to top. The panel boards are typically two or four inches high and four or five feet wide. Panel jumps can be made of wood or flexible plastic, but every board must be displaceable. It can also have wings. This jump is not used by all registries.

Jumping Basics

Horse trainers have a word for a correct jumping position. It is *bascule,* which refers to the round arc a horse's body makes as he goes over a jump. The horse should rise up through his back, stretching his neck forward and down as he reaches the peak of his jump. Theoretically, as he is over the jump, the horse takes the shape of a dolphin jumping out of the water. A horse with a good bascule has an extremely round jump, while a horse with a poor bascule jumps flat. A flat jumper has his head in the air and his back hollow. The hollow back prevents the horse from lowering his head and lifting his forearms, which blocks the tucking motion of the front legs to jump clear. A good bascule is an important trait for all horse-show jumpers, as it helps them to be more athletic over a jump and thus jump higher and cleaner. This same style of jumping is also seen with some agility dogs.

A Cavelier with a round jump.

On the other hand, steeplechase trainers prefer to see a flat jumper. In a steeplechase the hurdles or fences are meant to be brushed through, so it is detrimental for the horse to have a round jump. The round arc seen in horse-show jumpers sacrifices speed, which is unacceptable in a race. The time spent in the air neatly clearing the jump is a waste in a race, as is the energy output. Although its origins were closely tied to show jumping, agility is much closer to a steeplechase than a show jumping competition. Agility dogs typically jump flatter with their front legs extended, ready to drive forward fast and hard to the next obstacle.

Joe's Border collie, Argos, in a flat jump.

On an agility course, speed over the ground *and* through the air is critical. However, the dog must also clear the bars. Unlike steeplechasers, agility dogs cannot brush through the jumps. They must jump flat and fast like steeplechasers, but round and high enough to clear every bar.

Jump Styles

Dogs jump with a tremendous variety of styles, varying across breed and within breed. Any particular dog's skill at jumping depends on the dog's conformation, physical conditioning, and training. Although some dogs develop a true forearm tuck, most dogs simply flex their front legs flat, occasionally ending up in a flat line from head to tail.

Whether the dog jumps with his front legs extended or folded, the flat-line position allows the agility dog to land running, like a steeplechaser. The dog jumps with a wide-open or extended stride. However, equine steeplechasers do not jump on angles or over ascending spreads and do not jump a hurdle every twenty-five feet. Dogs must be flexible and quick on their feet to clear every bar, regardless of their speed, the angle of approach, or the width of the jump. The variable jumping conditions found on every agility course require that the agility dog also jump like a horse-show jumper. These highly trained horses maintain a

This Weimaraner is displaying a flat jump style.

short or collected stride for a takeoff position that is in close quarters to the jump. This allows for a well-rounded leap with lots of vertical height and a correct arc (or bascule). For agility dogs, collected jumping is necessary for handling jumps set at angles and around tight curves, both of which occur on agility courses from novice to masters. Being successful at both jump styles is why the sport is *agility,* based on the word *agile,* meaning "quick and well coordinated in movement."

Zoie lands on angle toward her handler.

Regardless of the style every jump has three components: takeoff, arc, and landing. A collected jump has a soft, rounded arc over the center of the hurdle. An extended jump has a flat curve over the center of the hurdle. Knocked bars occur when the dog takes off early, late, or too flat. An early takeoff means the dog is coming back down before he clears the bar. A late takeoff means the dog is still rising as he clears the bar. A flat jump means the dog did not give the bar enough clearance. Refer to the Jumping Basics diagram below.

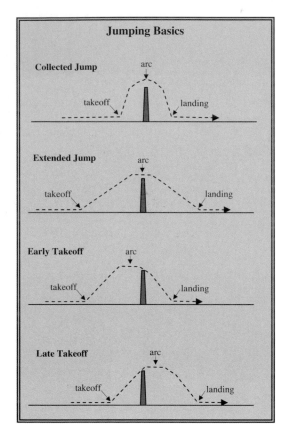

Agility dogs must be capable of jumping with a collected and extended stride. Teaching your dog both techniques is important. Most dogs favor one style or another, although there are exceptions in every breed. Border collies frequently jump flat, using their athleticism to clear the bar and skid through turns. Golden retrievers, poodles, and collies often have a beautiful, natural rounded jump. As you work through jump training, your dog's preference will become apparent and you can then tailor the training to your dog. Flat jumpers need more collection work. Well-collected dogs need more extension work. Achieving a balance will give you a coordinated, speedy dog.

Although it is a long process, teaching the correct takeoffs and jump positions from the beginning is critical. Remember: The sport of agility is 60 to 90 percent jumping.

Collected Jump Training

Although both jump styles (collected and extended) must be taught, it is easier to first shape and train a collected jump style. A jump with a round arc, or correctly located bascule, is harder to train than a flat leap. Shaping a correct arc takes longer, but the results are permanent and really only takes a few weeks before your dog is truly jumping.

If you rush your dog into jumping, simply because he can jump, you are forcing your dog to figure out the most important part of agility by himself.

The first component in collected jumping is the correct takeoff spot, which requires that the dog stride right up to the base of the jump. Approaching the jump many dogs simply launch at the hurdle. Athletic dogs may clear the bar, but a clean jump is a hit-or-miss deal. If the dog's striding was correct, or he put extra effort into the leap, then he clears the bar. If the dog mistimes his takeoff, taking off too close to the hurdle, he will bring down the bar with his front legs. Another takeoff timing error occurs when the dog takes off too early. This dog brings down the bar just as easily. For the untrained dog every jump

This Rotweiller took off too close to the jump, thus the jump arc is after the jump.

is an experiment of muscle and coordination. Furthermore, if the handler calls, moves, or distracts the dog during the jump, the bar comes down. This "lottery" style of jumping can make agility frustrating and expensive versus fun and entertaining.

At Mountain Freaks we shape the dog's jump style correctly, before bad habits develop. As your dog begins to truly jump the hurdle, he learns to balance and adjust his stride for a correct takeoff. For this reason, jump training requires multiple iterations of each exercise. Over the next several months, set aside five or ten minutes a few times a week to work on the following exercises. Proceed slowly and let your dog build his confidence before raising the bar—both literally and figuratively. Your practice jump can be purchased or homemade, like a wood dowel or PVC pipe on a stack of books. It does not matter so long as the bar can be knocked off if your dog does not jump correctly. For this same reason do not use an obedience panel jump. All the exercises should be done with one bar and on a soft surface. Never jump your dog on concrete, asphalt, or hard flooring like linoleum. Traction is important.

INTRODUCE THE COLLECTED JUMP

Shaping a collected jump, which has a takeoff point very close to the jump, encourages your dog to jump with a correct arc. The key component to shaping a soft arc is where the dog receives the reward. You must drop the reward on the ground directly below your dog's nose, close to the jump. In following or anticipating the treat, your dog's head will curve down and his hind quarters will lift. This naturally shapes his jump into an arc.

This golden jumps with tucked feet.

The tucked feet require that the dog leap higher to clear the bar and then untuck his feet prior to landing. Both actions can jeopardize a clean jump, and the dog wastes a lot of effort. All dogs can learn to jump with extended back feet (vs tucked). The effort and time involved to obtain a correct jump depend more on the handler's commitment than the dog's abilities.

Some breeds naturally tuck their rear feet under their bellies when they jump. Many hunting breeds like to jump into the water. It is part of their breeding, and they instinctively tuck their back feet to prevent a slapping belly flop! This also puts their legs in the perfect position to begin swimming. All of this is super if you are training for a hunt test—not so good in agility.

For this exercise use a simple jump (no wing) with a single bar. Kneel or sit on the floor at the end of the jump, facing the standard. Being close to the jump and low to the ground keeps your dog close to the jump too. Put the jump bar at one quarter your dog's jump height. Use a treat that plops versus one that rolls or bounces. Do not use a toy.

1. With your dog off the leash, let him wander over the bar. Mark with a click each time your dog passes over the bar. Reward. Mark only the passes over the bar that are clean. Your dog should never come into physical contact with any part of the bar or standard. This is important. Your dog needs to understand immediately that ticking or knocking a bar means no reward. Remember to drop the reward on the ground. Never reward from your hand.

Trouble Shooting: If your dog balks at the bar, lower it. Ideally you should use a jump that adjusts in two-inch increments.

2. Once your dog is successfully crossing over the bar in both directions and is freely offering a clean pass, raise the bar in two- or four-inch increments. Mark and reward only clean passes over the bar. In this drill it is your neutral response (no response, no reward) to a knocked bar that defines the behavior best for the dog. Continue to drop the reward at your dog's landing spot, which should be no more than two feet from the jump, even for large dogs.

Continue to gradually raise the bar until your dog is jumping full height. Repeat this exercise for multiple sessions, starting at whatever height you ended the previous training session. When your dog is freely offering a full-height jump and is keeping the bar up with a high (90 percent) success rate, repeat the process standing up.

SHAPE THE COLLECTED TAKEOFF

Once your dog understands the idea of jumping and is performing the introduction exercises at full height, you can add motion to shape a correct takeoff position. For this exercise you will toss the reward on the ground but one dog length away from the jump. This allows your dog to put in a stride before he turns around from picking up the first treat and jumps again. Toss the treat in a straight line, back and forth across the jump. Stand at one end of the jump, facing the bar. Use a single-bar, wingless jump.

1. Warm up with a few passes over the bar, as taught in the introduction. Mark each successful arc by dropping the reward on the ground at the landing spot.

2. After the third or fourth clean pass over the bar, wait for your dog to land and then toss the treat one dog length away from the jump (versus at the landing spot).

3. Let your dog eat the treat and turn naturally back to you. Let him offer the jump again. With a clean landing, toss the treat one dog length away from the jump on the opposite side.

Trouble Shooting: If your dog extends and takes off farther from the bar, do two drops, rewarding at the landing spot, to remind him to take off close to the bar.

This drill should not be done over the course of a day. With a full-grown dog, this process should be worked at intervals and spread over several days to two weeks when training daily.

Throughout the introduction and takeoff drills, you shaped your dog's ability to jump collected. Equally important, you also taught your dog that a knocked bar receives no reward. Knocking a bar does

Raise the bar as your dog ages. With young dogs you can continue with the exercises in this chapter, but do not raise the bar. Use the following age guidelines:

Less than nine months	no jumping
Nine to twelve months	bar no higher than three-quarters jump height
twelve months or more	bar to full height

not hurt nor does it scare or frighten most dogs at this level. With you being neutral (i.e., stationary and quiet), your dog is also not dealing with multiple sets of stimuli. It is simply dog vs jump. By rewarding only those passes over the jump that are clean, your dog can think about his job. You want your dog to clearly understand that a knocked bar equals no reward. By progressing slowly and carefully through these exercises, your dog's understanding of where to take off improves and he learns to keep his feet up.

Many dogs are natural born steeplechasers at heart and want to brush through the bars rather than clear them. If your dog is in this category, use these drills frequently through-out his agility career.

INCREASE THE DISTANCE

Jumping sounds simple, but the actual execution and training are more complex. The first step after the introduction is to get your dog to jump from a collected stride regardless of the distance or angle to the jump. Striding and balance are critical skills for an agility dog. As the distance between obstacles increases, your dog must learn to collect his stride before a jump in order to land turning. Landing softly requires the dog to take off close to the jump. He must also learn to approach hurdles from a variety of angles. In order for your dog to learn these skills, you need to shape his approach to the jump from a variety of distances.

For the following exercises continue to stand at the end of the jump, facing the standard. Start with the bar at your dog's full-jump height.

1. Warm up with a few passes over the bar, as taught in the introduction. Mark each successful arc by dropping the reward on the ground at the landing spot.

2. After the third or fourth clean landing, toss the treat two dog lengths away from the jump. Wait before tossing the treat to be sure your dog has completely landed. Let him turn naturally, and offer the jump again.

The dog takes off and lands close to the jump with a soft, rounded arc.

3. With a clean effort toss the treat two dog lengths away from the jump on the opposite side. Continue tossing the treat in a straight line. Picture a clock with the jump in the middle. Your dog should be jumping from twelve o'clock to six o'clock or six to twelve o'clock.

> **Trouble Shooting:** If your dog extends and takes off farther from the bar, do two repetitions where you drop the treat at the landing spot to remind him that the takeoff is close to the bar.

Through several sessions let your dog offer the jump. As he lands, toss the treat farther and farther away from the jump, up to three, four, or five dog lengths. Once your dog is successfully clearing the bar with several strides on either side of the jump, you can move on to angled approaches.

CHANGE THE JUMP ANGLE

Agility dogs frequently jump on an angle. An important part of jump training is to let your dog see and approach the jump from a variety of angles and distances. Stand at one end of the jump, facing the bar. Start with the bar at your dog's full-jump height.

1. Warm up with a few passes over the bar, as taught in the introduction. Mark each successful arc by dropping the reward on the ground at the landing spot.

2. After the third or fourth clean arc, toss the treat three dog lengths away from the jump, but toss it on a forty-five degree angle. Let him turn naturally and offer the jump again.

3. With a clean effort, toss the treat three dog lengths away from the jump on the opposite side but again on a forty-five-degree angle. Your dog is now slicing back and forth across the bar. Picture a clock with the jump in the mid-

dle. Your dog should be jumping from one o'clock to seven o'clock or from eleven to five o'clock.

Once your dog is jumping a clean full-height jump from a forty- or forty-five-degree angle, change his approach to thirty-five, thirty, or even twenty degrees. Picture a clock with the jump in the middle. Your dog should be jumping from two o'clock to eight o'clock or from ten to four o'clock.

CHANGE POSITIONS

For the introduction and shaping drills, you stood facing the jumping in a very neutral position. This allowed your dog to concentrate on the jump. Your stationary position kept you out of the picture. The next step is to change your position relative to your dog's. There are two ways to signal or cue your dog for a collected jump. You can remain on the takeoff side of the jump or you can be facing the jump on the landing side. On the takeoff side, you can be facing forward. It is your position behind the jump that cues your dog to turn or wrap back to you. On the landing side, you must be facing the jump.

For the following exercises, mark each successful landing and reward from the hand. Keep your hand low (below dog's head). Do several repetitions on either side.

- Stand on the *takeoff* side of the jump facing forward. Your shoulders, hips, and feet should be pointing in the direction your dog is jumping. Release dog forward and reward when he wraps back to you.

- Stand on the *landing* side of the jump with your body parallel to the standard. Let your dog jump to you and land softly

Being on the landing side of the jump is a powerful collected jump cue.

between you and the jump. Your dog should land with his body parallel to the jump bar. Refer to photos on this page.

This is also where we add a verbal command for jump. Common choices include *Over, Jump*, or *Bar*. We do not use the common obedience term *Hup*, simply because it takes too long to say and begins with a soft consonant.

COLLECTED JUMP: AROUND THE CLOCK

Throughout most of the introduction phase, you were always stationary. By remaining still, your dog learned to jump without interfacing with you. The second step was to show your dog the two body positions (behind the jump on takeoff and facing the jump on the landing side) that cue a collected jump. The next phase is to integrate motion into your dog's jump training by adding basic groundwork.

As you begin this next phase, it is extremely important to remain upright as you move. Do not bend or lean. Your upright, relaxed position is another visual cue for your dog to remain collected and jump softly. When you move onto longer jump sequences, this "picture" is important. You will be able to communicate to your dog the need for a collected jump or shortened stride by simply standing up!

The easiest ground drill to integrate with the collected jump is close. Use the same around-the-clock pattern found in the advanced close drills, but with a jump in the center of the clock. This drill has multiple components. It should be completed or repeated over the course of several weeks. Train in short five- or ten-minute sessions. For this drill a rotation contains five positions for the dog: twelve, eleven, ten, one, and two o'clock. A set contains multiple distances for the dog but only one distance for the handler. And each set must be done with the handler facing the dog and then facing the direction the dog is jumping. Remember to work on the left and the right sides.

Remember to reward wait. Multiple repetitions of the advanced drills can wear out your dog's wait, so reward frequently and with enthusiasm.

For the collected jump exercises, the handler stands in front of the jump.

SET A

The drill begins simply, with the dog sitting directly in front of the jump and the handler standing on the opposite side of the jump. The takeoff and landing distance should be equal to the height of the jump. For example, with a twenty-inch jump, the takeoff position for the dog is twenty inches away and the handler stands on the landing side of the jump about twenty inches away.

1. Place your dog at the twelve o'clock position and move to the opposite side of the jump. Your feet should be in an open stance, and your arm should be extended toward the jump and dog. Keep your eyes down your arm, connected to your dog.

2. Release your dog by saying "Okay. Jump." Do not move as your dog jumps. This is a collected jump drill, and your dog should land parallel to the jump. Reward the dog in the close position.

If your dog lands on you or beyond the close position, do not reward. Try again. Keep your arm low and lure your dog slowly over the jump. If he over-extends past close again, lower the bar by four or more inches so he can practice finding close a few times without having to jump high.

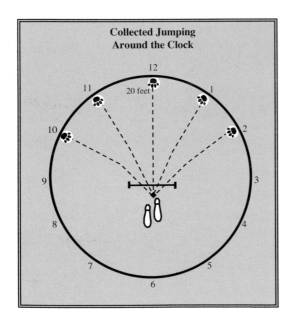

Collected Jumping
Around the Clock

Repeat with the dog at positions eleven and one o'clock and do both sides. Once your dog is jumping confidently and cleanly into you, move him back in one-foot increments to a distance of twenty feet. At each distance do all the positions (twelve, eleven, one, ten, and two o'clock). Do not change your distance.

Once you have worked through all the positions to

a distance of twenty feet, you can repeat the entire set but face forward. Even though you are facing forward, your dog should land in the close position. Do not move forward.

SET B

Using the basic around-the-clock pattern, you can now change the distance your dog travels to you after the jump. Every distance change encourages him to extend his stride, so do not move until your dog is landing quietly and easily in close. For this second set begin at twice the dog's jump height and then move gradually farther from the jump. For example, with a twenty-inch-high jump, you should be forty inches away from the jump. Repeat all the exercises in Set A, beginning with your dog directly in front of the jump and continuing to move the dog back in one-foot increments to about twenty feet. Remember to work both the left and right sides. Always reward your dog in close. After completing all the positions at maximum distance, repeat the set but move farther away from the jump (e.g., three times the jump height). Continue to gradually move away from the jump to a distance of about fifteen feet.

Once you have completed the set facing the dog, repeat it facing forward, in the direction the dog is jumping.

COLLECTED JUMPING: ON AN ANGLE

Another important skill for the dog is to jump on an angle. Dogs do not always approach a jump straight in agility. Mild angles were introduced in the around-the-clock drill. This next drill lets your dog practice striding over a jump at a much sharper angle, like fifteen and thirty degrees. The drill begins with the dog directly in front of the jump on a fifteen degree angle. You stand on the opposite side of the jump at a distance equal to your dog's jump height. You should be facing your dog.

1. Position the dog on a fifteen degree angle. Face the jump and extend your arm toward the dog. Eyes down your arm, connected to your dog.

2. Release your dog by saying "Okay. Jump." Do not move as your dog jumps.

3. Reward the dog in close position as he slices over the jump on an angle.

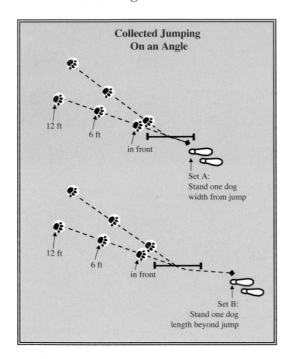

Collected Jumping On an Angle

12 ft
6 ft
in front

Set A:
Stand one dog
width from jump

12 ft
6 ft
in front

Set B:
Stand one dog
length beyond jump

With success—meaning a soft, controlled landing—gradually move your dog back in one-foot increments to a distance of about twenty feet. Repeat the rotation with your dog at a thirty-degree angle. The larger angle is actually harder as your dog moves away from the jump. You do not change your distance. Remember to work both the left and right sides. Always reward your dog in close. Once you have completed the set facing the dog, repeat both angles but face forward, in the direction the dog is jumping. At this level you should continue to use your dog's jump height as a distance marker for where you should be standing.

ADVANCED DRILLS

The following drills add obstacles and motion to the basic around-the-clock drill. Each drill will expand your dog's understanding of striding as he covers different distances and approaches the hurdle from different directions. These drills should be completed over several weeks. Train in five- or ten-minute sessions.

Moving Close

Repeat the around–the-clock drill, but this time go into motion when you call your dog over the jump. Move away smoothly and calmly at a walk. Maintain an open stance with your arm and shoulder turned toward your dog. Reward your dog when he reaches close position.

Add a Jump

Repeat the around-the-clock drill with two jumps. Set the jumps in the middle of the clock and at six o'clock. The jumps should be two times the jump height apart. For example, with a sixteen-inch jump, the two jumps should be thirty-two inches apart. This is the beginning of grid work. For each set in the drill, maintain the same distances from the jump but use two jumps. For example, for the first rotation in Set A, you should stand the jump height away from the second jump while your dog sits directly in front of the first jump. Always stand facing the jump for this drill. Do not move as the dog jumps and reward your dog at close.

Tunnel Play

Another easy collection drill uses a tunnel. Place a jump about two times the jump height in front of a short (six- or eight-foot) tunnel. Start with the bar eight inches below full height and work up to full height. Put the tunnel in a (-shape. Remember to work both the left and right sides.

For the first exercise send your dog into the tunnel and stand between the tunnel exit and the jump. For this drill you are signaling collection by remaining on the takeoff side of the jump. Let your dog jump the hurdle as he exits the tunnel. Reward in close.

The second exercise is the reverse. Send the dog over the jump and into the tunnel. The position of the tunnel encourages your dog to arc softly to duck quickly into the tunnel. Reward the dog in a moving close as he exits the tunnel. If your dog is extremely fast in the tunnel, use a deeper C-shape to give yourself time to get to the end of the tunnel.

Extended Jump Training

Once your dog has learned to take off and land with a correct arc, you can begin extended jump training. This does not mean your dog should begin flinging himself over jumps. Teaching your dog to stride through and over a hurdle requires equal time and effort.

You must give your dog practice at lengthening and shortening his stride—perhaps not as much as with collected work—but some. On an agility course every line or sequence of jumps contains variable distances and angles. Your dog must learn to lengthen and shorten his stride to handle different conditions.

> In between extended-jump drills, put in a few of the collected-jump drills. You want to keep reminding your dog how and when to collect.

Shaping an extended jump, which has a takeoff point farther away from the jump, is generally not necessary. This is most dogs' natural style. Remember shaping is a tool to get your dog to offer a behavior. If the dog offers the behavior naturally, it does not need to be shaped. What you do need is give your dog practice through a variety of jump chutes with different distances and angles.

Jump chutes and circles encourage your dog to jump flatter and land running. Your dog's cue to do this is when you pass the jump. Therefore, for the following drills, you—the handler—are an integral part of the exercises, since your motion and position reinforce his striding.

JUMP CHUTES

There are a wide variety of exercises that can be done with a few jumps. All of the following use four jumps in a straight line, also referred to as a chute. Use single bar, wingless jumps. Refer to the Extended Jumping: Jump Chutes diagram on page 137. Set the bars four inches below your dog's normal height.

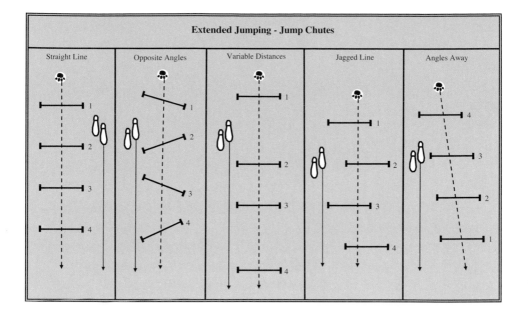

Straight Line

The first jump chute uses four jumps in a straight line. The jumps should be set about fifteen feet apart. To introduce the concept of jump lines, this drill uses backchaining. In a backchain exercise, you do the last obstacle first, then the last two, etc., thus proceeding backward to the beginning. The last piece of the exercise is all four jumps.

To begin this exercise, position your dog in front of jump 4. Move to the side of the jump. Stand parallel to the jump and release the dog over the jump. Move forward with the release and reward dog in close. For the next rep, position your dog in front of jump 3. Stand between jumps 3 and 4. Do not get inside the line of jumps. Your line of motion should not be impeded. Release the dog over jump 3 and move forward with the dog as he takes jump 4. Keep moving forward on a slight curve (away from the jump line) and reward your dog when he reaches close. For the next rep begin with jump 2, and then for the final rep, begin with jump 1. Move forward gently with the dog as he takes the jumps. Do not race off at full speed. Keep moving forward but at a steady fast trot or walk. Try to pace your dog rather than race him. Vary your start position and remember to work both the right and left sides.

Opposite Angles

Another variation is to set the jumps on a slight angle. You can angle all the jumps in the same direction, keeping the center of the jumps aligned, or you can angle every other jump, as shown in the diagram. Keep the jumps the same distance apart. This encourages the dog to jump straight regardless of the jump's angle. Notice that the dog's path through the jumps is a straight line, as is the handler's. Do not zigzag between the jumps. Move to the side and travel straight. Work both the left and right sides.

Trouble Shooting: If your dog knocks a bar, stop immediately. Call your dog back and put him in a sit or down while you reset the bar. This brief time-out is important. Your dog needs to understand that knocked bars (a) end the game and (b) eliminate any possibility of a reward. Send the dog back over the jump he knocked. If he lands clean, verbally praise and reward him with a treat. Repeat the previous exercise.

Trouble Shooting: If your dog takes the line faster than you, take a larger head start or lead out.

Variable Distances

The first two drills kept the jumps at the same distance. This allowed your dog to look at a variety of jump configurations but kept his striding the same. This drill requires multiple stride changes. Move the jumps farther apart, up to twenty-five feet apart, but do not move them closer than eight feet. Every other pass down the line, vary the distances between jumps so he cannot memorize their location.

Jagged Line

Once your dog understands how to take a short line of jumps with different angles and distances, vary the position of the jumps on the line. Keep the jumps perpendicular to the dog's path and at the same distance apart. Move the jumps a few feet right or left of the center line.

This encourages the dog to jump either side of the jump, not just the center. It also puts you, the handler, farther away from the dog's line. Keep working both sides and vary your starting point.

> **Trouble Shooting:** If your dog cuts into you between jumps, remember to extend your arm and use an *Out* command to keep your dog secure at a distance. Do a few groundwork exercises with a wing.

Angles Away

With your dog moving confidently through a line of four jumps, you can wean him off your position even more. There are two pieces to this drill. First, set the jumps back in a straight line with a regular distance between the jumps. Run the dog up and down the line a few times. With each pass move farther from the line of jumps. This is referred to as lateral distance. As your distance (laterally) from the jump line increases, remember to keep your arm extended, which tells your dog to stay on his line even though yours is changing. The second part of the drill is to set the jumps in a lateral, ascending line away from you. In this configuration you maintain a straight path but your dog continues to move laterally away from you. Keep working both sides and vary your starting point.

> Once you begin working lines with variable distances or circles, your dog may knock more bars. This is a normal part of his learning curve. At this point he is adjusting his stride to find the correct takeoff point. Practice helps.

Add Wings

Repeat the line drills with wing jumps, which force more distance between you and the dog. Many small dogs are more sensitive to this distance than large dogs. Depending on the size of the wing, the wing may also interrupt the dog's view of you.

JUMP CIRCLES

The jump circle is the beginning of sequence training. As you work through the following drills, remember that you are working with your dog. Even with simple drills, teamwork is important. Jump circles also allow you to further integrate your groundwork training. These drills provide lots of exercise for your dog and should be done over the course of weeks. Train in five-minute sessions.

Simple Circle

The simplest configuration is six jumps set in a fifteen-foot-diameter circle. Use six wingless, single bar jumps. Think of a clock. The jumps are located at one, three, five, seven, nine, and eleven o'clock. Position the dog directly in front of the jump at one o'clock. Move ahead (lead out) between jumps and face forward. Connect with the dog, release him over the jump, and then continue around all the jumps. *Always* move with your dog. It is important for you to be even with or ahead of your dog around the circle. Give a clear *Jump* command for each jump in the circle. After the last jump, at eleven o'clock, move to the center of the circle and call your dog to *Close*. Work the circle left and right.

Troubleshooting **If your dog knocks a bar, stop immediately. Call your dog back and put him in a sit or down while you reset the bar. This brief time-out is important. Your dog needs to understand that knocked bars (a) end the game and (b) eliminate any possibility of a reward. Send the dog back over the one jump he knocked. If he lands clean, verbally praise and reward. Repeat the exercise.**

You can also send the dog around the jump circle while gently spiraling your path in. Use an *Out* command to keep your dog secure at a distance. To keep your dog from memorizing the strides, expand the circle to twenty or twenty-five feet and then shrink back to fifteen feet.

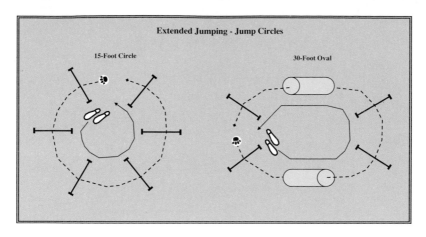

Extended Jumping - Jump Circles

15-Foot Circle

30-Foot Oval

Expand to an Oval

Elongate the circle into a thirty-foot oval with the jumps scattered at a variety of distances. Change the jump locations every few times your dog goes around the oval so he has to adjust his stride to keep jumping clean.

Integrate Tunnels

Tunnels, particularly laid straight or in a shallow C, encourage most dogs to keep their stride extended. This means more adjustments to clear all the jumps. Once your dog is successfully keeping the bars up around the jump oval, begin adding tunnels. Try the following:

- Replace the jumps at the short end of the oval with a (-shaped tunnel.

- Replace the jumps along one long side of the oval with a straight tunnel.

- Replace the jumps on both longs sides of the oval with straight tunnels. Thus the jumps are clustered at either end.

- Alternate jump, tunnel, jump all the way around the oval. With each pass around the circle, vary the distances between the jumps and tunnels.

- Replace the straight tunnel with a chute.

ADVANCED JUMP DRILLS

Once your dog can work a circle of jumps, you can begin to add more handling commands. A large part of line and circle work is to get your dog to take the obstacle in front of him. A key rule here is "so long as you are moving forward also." If you stop, your dog should come to close, which is why it is critical for you to keep moving—particularly your arm and hand—while your dog jumps around you. *Never* stand completely stationary. Your shoulder, arm, and hand should be "drawing" the dog's path even if you are not traveling the same distance as the dog.

Use the following exercises to keep your dog in sync with your handling. All of these use a standard six-jump oval.

Interrupt the Circle

Send your dog over the first three jumps and call to *Close*. To do this you must ease your pace and let your dog jump ahead of you at the third jump. Your pace change should cue him that the path is changing. Stand up and gently rotate your shoulder in a U-turn into the center of the circle. Standing up is another cue for your dog to collect and change directions. Your shoulder rotation "draws" the new path and the call to *Close* tells your dog where you want him.

> **Trouble Shooting:** If your dog continues around the circle, do several U-turns on the flat to focus his attention on your shoulder motions rather than the obstacles. Then do the U-turn over one jump, then over two jumps. As your dog begins to develop obstacle focus (which means he focuses on the next obstacle or choice of obstacles), it is important to keep reminding him to follow your body language cues also.

Once your dog is keying in on your shoulder motion, try the exercise at various locations on the oval. For example, send him over five jumps before calling to *Close* or send him over only the first two jumps. Remember to work both the right and left sides.

Alter Your Path

Send your dog around the six jumps laid out in an oval, but shrink your path in the center. This is similar to the Angles Away exercise you did on a jump line. Remember to keep your arm extended to support your dog on his path, while you alter yours. And use an *Out* command. You must also continue rotating. Even if your path is shorter, your arm and shoulder should remain connected to your dog. Do not stand in the center and watch.

Jump vs Wait

Another excellent groundwork drill is to put the dog in a wait or stay at the start of a jump circle. Rework the wait drills (i.e., walk in front, bend down to tie shoe, walk a circle around him). Release the dog and send him around the oval with alternate jumps and tunnels and then immediately repeat wait drills.

Jump vs Close

Another excellent drill with jump oval is to walk your dog in a close around the center of the circle. Every once in awhile, select a jump and send your dog over. Immediately call your dog back to *Close* and resume moving around the circle. The critical skill here is that the dog cannot take an obstacle until you ask (aka signal) for it. Use close, back, and a few U-turns to vary your path and keep your dog's attention on your hand. Start with a very large thirty-foot circle and shrink it slowly. You can also weave between jumps. Keep your hand low and close to your side. Repeat close and reward frequently to reassure your dog that he is correct to stay with you.

Grid Work

A grid of jumps or bounce work is an important tool for collected jumping. The basic configuration is three jumps set two times the jump height apart. Grid work exercises provide the dog with lots of practice on finding the takeoff spot. The purpose is to get your dog to completely collect. In other words, he lands and then takesoff from the same spot. Think of a dolphin leaping out of the water and arcing right back in. Your dog should arc fluidly over all three jumps. These exercises are, however, hard work, so do them in very short sessions.

INTRODUCE THE GRID

Set out three wingless, single-bar jumps. The jumps should be set at half your dog's regular height and should be spaced approximately two times the jump height apart. This gives your dog just enough room to land, collect, and take off. In the collection grid there are no strides between jumps, which can definitely surprise dogs with a natural tendency to jump big. Regardless of your dog's jumping style, for safety we introduce the dog to the collection grid by backchaining the sequence. This minimizes your motion, which encourages your dog to stay collected.

With a three-jump grid, the handler stands to the side, between jumps 2 and 3, and lets the dog wrap back to close.

1. Sit the dog behind jump 3.

2. Stand on the takeoff side of the jump, facing the direction the dog is jumping. Release the dog over the jump. If he clears the bars, call to *Close* and reward. If not, regroup and try again.

3. Sit the dog behind jump 2.

4. Stand to the side about halfway between jumps 2 and 3. Face the direction the dog is jumping. Release the dog over the jumps. Call to *Close* and reward.

5. Sit the dog behind jump 1.

6. Stand to the side about halfway between jumps 2 and 3. Face the direction the dog is jumping. Release the dog over all three jumps. Call to *Close* and reward.

Trouble Shooting: If your dog knocks bars, let him retry once. If he knocks the bar again, move back one step in the exercise. You can also lower the height for one repetition.

Grid work should be done on both the right and left sides. With each successful pass through the three-jump grid, raise the bars two or four inches. You can also use ascending heights (first jump low, second jump a little higher, third jump highest) and then raise the first and second jump heights with each successful pass through the grid. Once the dog is working at full height, you can recall the dog to close through the grid. Stand to the side of jump 3.

A three-jump grid is a collection exercise.

ADD HANDLER MOTION

Once your dog becomes proficient at grid work or bouncing, you should begin to vary where you stand, when you go into motion, and how fast you move. At this point your dog must learn to jump correctly regardless of your motion. If you move forward while he is jumping, he cannot change his stride to match yours. If he does, he will knock bars. This is discipline. He must learn to manage his stride for the jump regardless of where you are or what you are doing. This takes practice, particularly for high-drive dogs.

During the introduction the handler stands between jumps 2 and 3 and remains stationary while the dog jumps. This neutral position allows the dog to concentrate on his job. In this drill you begin to move. By adding motion in tiny increments, you allow your dog to learn and, at the same time, desensitize him to your motion. Many dogs jump well and move through these drills easily. Others require months of practice. This drill should be done on the left and right sides.

1. Place the dog directly in front of jump 1. Stand to the side of the grid, about halfway between jumps 1 and 2 and face the direction the dog is jumping. Release your dog over jump 1 and walk forward gently (quiet body language). Reward in close after the last jump. Do not walk past jump 3 (collection cue).

2. Repeat the drill but stand to the side of the grid, halfway between the dog and jump 1.

> **Trouble Shooting:** If your dog knocks a bar, retry once. If he knocks the bar again, change one criterion for the next attempt: stand between jumps 2 and 3, walk slower, or lower the jump height.

INCREASE THE DOG'S STARTING DISTANCE

The next step is to give the dog more momentum heading into the grid. This is where the dog must learn to regulate his stride. Be patient and calm through these drills. Particularly for high-drive dogs, this is a very difficult skill to master.

With successive reps through the grid, move your dog back in one-foot increments, up to about twenty feet. You should always stand to the side of jumps 2 and 3 facing forward or on the landing side of jump 3 facing the jumps. Always reward in close.

ADD A TUNNEL

Repeat the introduce-the-grid drill but with a straight tunnel. Begin with the tunnel exit set at a distance equal to two times the jump height. Shrink the tunnel to about six feet and use a reduced jump height. Racing through a straight tunnel allows your dog to extend his stride. Bouncing the grid requires that he collect and balance immediately. With each successful pass through the grid, extend the tunnel a few feet until the dog is executing a full-length tunnel. Move the tunnel back in one-foot increments until the tunnel exit is twenty feet away for the first jump in the grid. You should always stand to the side of jumps 2 and 3 facing forward or on the landing side of jump 3 facing the jumps. Always reward in close.

Single-Jump Drills

With limited space and a single jump, you can let your dog practice jumping while you integrate his groundwork training. These drills ensure that your dog is watching you for direction and is focused on your hand and arm signals. They reinforce the four directionals (motion, focus, hand, and voice) and begin to expand his understanding of which directional to respond to. Remember to work all these exercises on both sides.

Many of these jump drills make good warm-up exercises for pre-course work. And they are helpful for introducing different or unusual surfaces, such as mats, indoor turf, or carpets.

U-TURN

The U-turn guides your dog up to, over, and around a jump in a gentle U-shape. For this exercise he is following your motion.

1. Put your dog twelve to fifteen feet away from the jump. You should remain next to your dog.

2. Release the dog over the jump and move forward a few feet with him. As the dog commits to the jump, gently roll your arm and shoulder into a U-turn to encourage your dog to turn. Your arm and shoulder are drawing the curve. Stay connected to your dog but do not pass the jump yourself.

3. As your dog lands, calmly call his name, followed by *Close*. Reward in close position.

CREATIVE FLOWS

With one jump and your basic groundwork commands (*Close*, *Out*, and *Back*), you can create multiple paths for your dog to follow. Be creative and give your dog practice following your hand through a curve or turn and then relocating the correct takeoff point for the jump. Try the following:

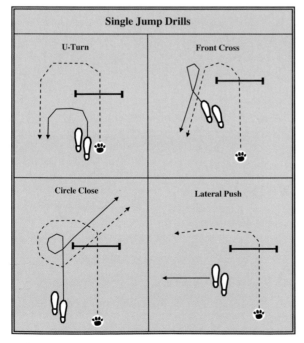

Single Jump Drills

U-Turn — Front Cross — Circle Close — Lateral Push

Simple Front Cross

Put your dog twelve to fifteen feet away from the jump. Lead out halfway to the jump. Release the dog over the jump and move

forward a few feet with him. As
the dog takes off, gently turn into
the dog and show him a clear hand
switch. As the dog lands, complete
your own rotation and call the dog
to *Close*. Reward.

Circle Close

Put your dog fifteen feet away
from the jump. Remain next to
him but to the side. Your path
past the jump must be clear (i.e.,
do not get stuck behind the jump
or wing). Release the dog over the
jump and move forward past the
jump with him. As the dog lands,
draw him to close and into a tight
circle. As your dog curves through
the circle, send him over the jump
a second time on an angle. As
your dog lands after the second
pass over the jump, move forward
past the jump and reward the dog
in close.

LATERAL PUSH

This exercise is an extension of out.
It requires that your dog commit
to the jump while you are moving
away on a lateral line. Although

The lateral push is an extension of out.

he must pick up and commit to an independent path, your dog is
supported by your hand and a verbal command. During this drill it
is important that you look at your dog and where he is going. Since
your shoulders and hips remain on a flat line, it is your hand signal
and voice that reassure your dog that he is correct.

1. Warm up with a few out groundwork drills.

2. Put dog fifteen feet from the jump.

3. Stand halfway between your dog and the jump and even with the stanchion.

4. Extend your hand toward the dog (not the jump). Release dog to jump while you step to the side. Do not rotate your shoulder toward the jump. Throughout this exercise your hand should point at the spot from which the dog left.

Trouble Shooting: If your dog does not move forward or moves toward you instead of to the jump, put a toy on the landing side, about one foot in front and to the side of the dog's turn. This will encourage his motion over the jump.

5. Move sideways as your dog moves toward the jump. A lateral line requires that your feet cross (left over right or right over left). Move on a line sideways. Do not pass the jump.

Trouble Shooting: If you cannot resist moving forward toward the jump, place a pole on the ground. Step sideways along the pole to guide your path. Keep your shoulders parallel to the pole.

With this drill, reward placement is critical. If you are working to get your dog committed to the jump, throw the reward in front and to the side where your dog is turning. This encourages the dog to move away. If you are working to keep your dog's focus (i.e., he is jumping too far), then collect the dog in close on your side of the jump. Keep moving sideways until he reaches close.

Equipment Specifics

Every type of jump has a nuance or special consideration. Although the introduction and early shaping drills vary depending on the type of jump, it is not necessary to repeat every drill for every type of jump. However, every jump should be trained before it is used in a sequence. Having been through the training on a single, wingless jump, your dog can often fast-forward through many of the drills on the different jump styles. Use the following training modifications and guides to determine which pieces of the jump drills work best for which jump type.

TIRE JUMP

The tire jump presents the dog with a twenty- or twenty-four-inch circle through which he must jump. Furthermore, the circle is suspended in the middle of the jump frame. This also presents the dog with multiple options. Rather than jump through the tire, many dogs try to go under or squeeze between the tire and the frame. The tire frame also allows the tire to swing, which some dogs find disturbing.

To prevent difficulties during course work, keep the following in mind when training the tire jump:

- When introducing the tire jump, put the tire on the ground and let your dog wander back and forth through the tire. This prevents it from swinging and gets your dog thinking about going through rather than under.

> **Trouble Shooting:** If your dog goes between the tire and frame, sit or stand directly in front of the tire. Put your hand through the tire and draw your dog to you. Mark each pass through the center. With multiple correct passes through the tire, slowly shift around until you are facing the direction your dog is moving, but stay in front of the tire until your dog is consistently moving through the center.

- You can also take the tire out of the frame and secure it between two wingless jump standards. This gives the dog fewer options with regards to completing the obstacle and teaches him to focus on the tire not the frame.

- Jumping through a tire is different on an angle. Approaching on a slant, the dog does not see the center. So he goes around or between the tire and frame. Give your dog practice seeing the tire at different distances and angles by using the tire jump in the collected-jumping—around-the-clock drill on pages 131–133. Simply replace the wingless, single bar with the tire.

PANEL

The panel jump consists of solid four-inch boards. Although this jump is the same height as the regular single-bar jump, it appears different to the dog. It looks solid, and many dogs think it is a bigger jump. Adding wings to a panel jump aggravates this assumption. To prevent problems during course work, the panel jump should be trained with all the basic collection and extension jump drills.

Another component to the panel jump is that dogs cannot see through it to the next obstacle. With a single-bar or even double-bar jump, your dog's line of sight is not impaired and he can see the next obstacle. Jumping over a panel jump, particularly one with large wings, your dog is blind to both the landing and the next obstacle. Keep this in mind when you call out obstacles during course work.

SPREAD JUMPS

There are three common spread jumps: double, triple, and broad. Introduce each of these jumps at very low heights and only after the dog has worked through the collected- and extended-jump drills (on page 130) over a single bar. Each type presents its own training issues.

Double

The double jump has two bars set apart at half the distance of the height. Thus a twelve-inch-high double jump has the top two bars set six inches apart. This means your dog must elongate his arc to cover the extra inches. Thus the double jump should be introduced with an extended stride.

Another consideration for the double jump is the dog's vision of the jump. Approaching the double jump, your dog cannot see both bars. He has no way of knowing that the jump he is approaching is a double. Get down to the dog's height and look at the double. The bars are parallel, and thus the second bar is invisible. However, most registries use two crossed bars beneath the parallel bars. With the crossed bars the dog can readily identify the double jump, so he can elongate the arc of his jump to clear both bars.

During the introduction it is also helpful to set the first bar (closest to the dog) two or four inches below the back bar. This creates an ascending double versus the parallel double used in competition. An ascending configuration allows your dog to see both bars. He can adjust to jumping a wider jump while you add a verbal, and then you can school him over parallel bars.

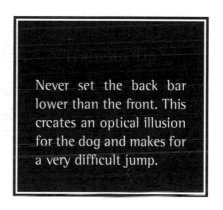

Never set the back bar lower than the front. This creates an optical illusion for the dog and makes for a very difficult jump.

Spread jumps are only taken in one direction, so do not ask your dog to jump back and forth as in the introduction exercises. Begin with the collected jumping practice exercises and be careful to toss at the landing spot. Once your dog is working reliably over the double, use the following as practice drills:

1. Simple Jump Line: Replace the second, third, or fourth jump with a double.

2. Jump Oval: Replace one of the six jumps with a double.

Single Jump: U-turn

4. Single Jump: Creative flows

It is also very important to work angled approaches. A double jump requires a longer arc. Approached and jumped on an angle, the width of the double jump increases. Use Sets B and C in the collected-jumping–around-the-clock drill (on page 132) to give your dog practice with angled approaches.

Triple

The triple jump is an ascending oxer, which means the jump has both height and width. For example, a sixteen-inch triple has three bars set at eight, twelve, and sixteen inches, with a spread of sixteen inches. The dog must jump high and wide.

The triple jump has both height and width.

The appearance of the triple jump can be tricky, particularly for small dogs. Most triple jumps are built with the bars descending from the rear versus ascending from the front. Thus the twenty-four-inch bars cover the entire frame of the jump, but the eight-inch bars are recessed in the frame. This means small dogs (those who jump eight and twelve inches) have a takeoff spot that is inside the frame of the jump.

Begin with the standard introduction jump exercises, but set the bars low. Once your dog is working reliably over the triple, use the following as practice drills:

1. Simple Jump Line: Replace the second, third, or fourth jump with a triple.

2. Jump Oval: Replace one of the six jumps with a triple.

3. Single Jump: U-turn

4. Single Jump: Creative flows

With beginner dogs work the triple jump on angles at very low heights. Gradually increase the height as the dog gains confidence. In fact, most registries do not use the triple in the novice or beginner classes.

Broad

The broad jump is a long jump. Flat boards, raised just a few inches off the ground, tempt many dogs to walk across the boards or step between them. Jumping the broad jump is not intuitive. It looks more like a pier or deck than a jump! The broad jump boards are all six to eight inches wide and are spread twice the dog's jump height. For example, for the twenty-inch jump height, the broad jump is set at forty inches. The number of boards varies from one to four, depending on the width and the registry.

Rather than school the broad jump as a different kind of jump, use your dog's training on the single-bar hurdle.

1. Set up a single-bar, wingless jump at eight inches for small dogs and twelve inches for medium and large dogs. Put the first broad-jump board directly in front of the bar (on the takeoff side). Use the lowest board.

2. Release the dog over the jump and mark each pass over both the bar and the board. Your dog can go in only one direction, but he should jump straight. Move forward past the jump and reward your dog in a moving close.

3. Add another broad-jump board. Put the second board directly behind the wingless jump. Your broad jump is now configured as: broad-jump board, jump, broad-jump board. Release the dog over the jump and mark each pass over both bars and the boards.

For small dogs that use only two boards, spread the boards to the correct distance after a few reps. For medium and large dogs, repeat the exercise with additional boards. Add a board to the front and then to the back. Mark correct passes over the bars and boards until the dog is jumping cleanly. The final step removes the wingless jump from the middle and places the broad jump stanchions on the corners.

Jump training is also a career long process. So long as you are competing, you should be jump training. A solid foundation keeps the exercises fun, and the drills become refresher courses. Periodic, strategic reviews of these drills will keep your dog's jumping skills sharp, particularly when you move on to short sequences and full course work. Speed also deteriorates many dogs' jumping skills. If bars start to come down, review the drills and correct—before you have major problems.

CHAPTER 9

Contact Obstacles

Agility requires that your dog be able to safely and quickly cross the dog walk, scramble over the A-frame, navigate the seesaw, and halt on the table. All four pieces of equipment—dog walk, A-frame, seesaw, and table—are considered contact obstacles. Almost every registry requires that the dog complete all four contact obstacles on a standard or regular course, even at the novice or beginner level.

Furthermore, dogs must also step on or through the contact zones, which are the first and last thirty or forty inches on the obstacle. The safety area or zone is highlighted on the contacts with an offsetting color, typically yellow or white. Zone performance is dictated by the registries for the safety of the dogs. The dogs must step in the contact zone on the up and down ramps of the dog walk. They must also step in the zone on the up and down sides of the seesaw. And the dogs must step in the down zone on the A-frame and, depending on the registry, sometimes also in the up zone. All this, plus the ability to navigate the actual piece of equipment, makes contact training time consuming. It also requires access to the equipment.

It is, however, the zone performance that requires the most time and attention. Once they are familiar with the equipment, dogs like to leap on and leap off. Though not particularly safe, sometimes it is simply a matter of stride and speed. But on occasion it is just more fun to leap!

Contact-Training Methodologies

There are numerous ways to teach agility dogs to keep their paws glued to the obstacle through the yellow zone, which ensures the dog's safety and is required for a clean performance. Each training method has specific advantages and disadvantages.

TWO–ON–TWO–OFF METHOD

One of the most common methods is the two-on-two-off (2-on-2-off) method. With this method the dog races across the contact and stops at the end with two front paws on the ground and two rear paws on the bottom of the contact. It is relatively easy to train, and you can use this method on all three obstacles (dog walk, A-frame, seesaw). The dog stops and waits for his handler to send him to the next obstacle. The time spent waiting is often balanced by a clearer, more direct line to the next obstacle. Furthermore, with a stopped contact, the handler gets a chance to catch up or regroup before continuing. However, the collection needed to stop, particularly on the A-frame, can strain the dog's shoulders and injure toes as the dog's paws pound into the slats.

A 2-on-2-off wait on the contacts allows the handler to catch up.

FOUR ON THE GROUND

Four paws on the ground is a simple variation of the 2-on-2-off method. Coming to a complete halt at the end of a contact requires tremendous physical effort, particularly for large or long-backed dogs. The angle of the A-frame increases the difficulty. To minimize the risk of injuries and protect the dog, many trainers choose to let the dog run off the end of the contact and stop on level ground. This is often referred to as four-on-the-ground (4-on-the-ground). Dogs can be trained to stop in a stand or in a down, but they always have four paws on the ground.

QUICK RELEASE

A quick release is not a method. It is the timing of the release with any stopped behavior trained at the bottom of an obstacle, such as a 2-on-2-off or 4-on-the-ground stop. Rather than hold the dog in position, the handler releases the dog immediately. Imbedded in the quick release is the intent to stop, even if for a fraction of a second. This provides the handler with control without sacrificing speed. Although the dog collects for the stop, the handler has the ability to send the dog on almost instantly, after the dog has stopped in the appropriate position.

RUNNING CONTACT

A moving or running contact allows the dog to run through or off the end of the board. Across the contact obstacle the dog remains in a completely extended stride. There is no collection or shortening of the stride. A variation of the running contact is a moving contact. With a moving contact the dog has a fully extended stride on the up ramp and across the middle board but collects on the down ramp. There is, however, no stop. With both running and moving contacts, the dog remains in motion. This is the most time-consuming method to train and requires a higher degree of fitness and commitment from both dog and handler. It also requires access to equipment four or five times a week. Furthermore, running contacts require the dog to understand directions (*Left, Right,* and *Go*) and be capable of performing and staying on course as directed, regardless of where the handler is or is going. In addition it requires precision and consistency from the handler, both in training and in execution. Running contacts are used for the dog walk and A-frame, never the seesaw. It is possible to train a running A-frame and a stopped dog walk. This is an option for slower handlers with fast dogs, because it is easier to get to the end of the A-frame than it is to get to the end of a thirty-six-foot dog walk.

With a running contact, the dog extends across the entire dog walk. (Photo courtesy of Joe Canova)

For safety Mountain Freaks teaches beginner students the dog walk, A-frame, and seesaw with a stop at the bottom. We believe the 2-on-2-off method provides consistency throughout the training and is relatively easy for both the dog and handler to learn. Many of our students begin with a stopped contact and then progress to a quick release as the team advances through to the higher levels of competition.

Equipment Introduction

The first stage of training is to introduce the dog to the basic agility equipment. For puppies under six months, contact training stops there. For older dogs the second stage is to introduce the A-frame and dog walk at very low heights. The goal throughout the contact introduction phase is to teach the dog to control its paws and navigate across the planks. You should not look for any specific behavior at the bottom of the plank. For the seesaw, we do a very gentle, slow progression that allows the dogs to adjust to the motion of the board long before we ask them to navigate across the entire obstacle, since most dogs are alarmed by a plank dropping under their paws.

INTRODUCE THE PAUSE TABLE

The pause table is truly a table, typically three feet by three feet. There are multiple heights, but eight, twelve, sixteen, and twenty-four inches are the most common. It is the easiest obstacle to introduce. It also lets your dog get used to the feel of the gritted agility surface without worrying about inclines or motion. Use a low table relative to your dog's height: an eight-inch table for puppies and dogs up to eighteen inches high; a sixteen-inch table for all other dogs.

1. Put your dog on the table.

2. Let him get used to the surface and the area. Ask for a sit or down. Get him to turn around. Play a gentle game of tug. Let him jump off.

3. Tap the table and get your dog to jump on and off a few times. Always ask for a sit or down once your dog is on the table.

INTRODUCE THE A-FRAME

Constructed of wood or aluminum, the A-frame consists of two ramps, typically nine feet long and three or four feet wide, which form an A shape. The apex of the A-frame varies across registries with five feet, six inches being common, though the USDAA Championship program uses a five-foot, ten-inch A-frame for the twenty-six-inch division. The contact or yellow zone is the last forty-two inches. For most registries the dog must clearly touch the contact zone with one paw. USDAA requires a foot in the contact zone on both the up and down ramps.

We prefer to introduce the A-frame before the dog walk since it is wider and easier for the dogs to navigate than the narrow dog walk. The goal is to get your dog moving comfortably over the A-frame. This is another good spot to let your dog watch first before trying. Remember that this is an introduction, not training. Let your dog practice running over the A-frame once or twice and then stop. Since the ultimate goal is to teach your dog to stop at the end of the down ramp, you do not want your dog to practice leaping off the end.

1. Set the A-frame at a very low height, about three feet at the apex.

2. Put your dog on the down side of the A-frame about three feet from the end, at the edge of the yellow zone. Release and let the dog gently move down the A-frame. Toss a reward forward or reward from your hand once the dog has all four paws on the ground.

Trouble Shooting: If your dog is too heavy to pick up, place the table next to the A-frame. Have your dog jump on the table and then walk down the A-frame. Start with a sixteen-inch table and then switch to the twenty-four-inch table. This gives your dog practice navigating the ramp. We also use a slightly lower (e.g., two-foot-high) A-frame for the dog's introductory passes.

3. Backchain in short increments, about one slat, with each repetition until your dog is moving over the entire A-frame.

Trouble Shooting: If your dog creeps up the ramp, use a tasty treat to lure him up. Do not give him the reward until he has crossed the apex. Your goal is to help your dog keep his momentum as he climbs the up ramp.

INTRODUCE THE DOG WALK

Constructed of wood or metal planks, the dog walk has three, twelve-foot planks. The middle plank of the dog walk is typically four feet high. The up and down ramps have slats for traction and a contact or yellow zone that is typically thirty-six inches long. In all registries the dog must put at least one foot in the contact zone on both the up and down planks.

Once your dog is willing to cross the low A-frame, you can move on to the narrower dog walk. Because the dog-walk plank is only twelve inches wide, for safety reasons there are multiple steps to this introduction.

Walk the Plank

Your goal is to get your dog moving confidently with balance down the entire plank, stepping on and exiting straight. You are also letting your dog practice controlling his paws, especially the rear, so he can keep his body straight. Twisting his body unbalances the dog on the plank, which can be dangerous on a full-height dog walk. Your dog is also getting used to the sounds and feel of a piece of agility equipment.

We start young puppies on a plank on the ground.

For this exercise lay the middle dog-walk plank (no slats) on level ground and sit or kneel next to the plank.

1. Let your dog step on, walk horizontally across, and turn around on the plank. Reward frequently and be patient while your dog figures out how to get all four paws on a twelve-inch wide board.

2. Once he is stepping on the board, stand up and guide him along the board. It is not necessary to start immediately from the end. You can guide him onto the plank on an angle.

3. Reward with a treat from the inside hand whenever you dog has four paws on the board, but always reward while the dog is in motion.

Raise the Plank

Once your dog can trot smoothly across the plank on the ground, start raising it in slow increments using the table. Always begin by guiding your dog onto the plank on a straight line. Reward with the inside hand while your dog is in motion. This rewards him for being in motion and keeps him from leaping or stepping on/off the plank. Remember to work both the left and right sides.

- LOW TABLE
  Put one end of the plank on the low eight-inch-high table. Let your dog walk up the plank to the table, turn around, and then walk back down. Next have your dog jump on the table and walk down. And finally walk your dog onto the middle of the plank. Approach on an angle, facing the bottom of the plank. You can tap the board to encourage him to jump on and walk down. Putting your dog on the plank in the middle lets him practice getting his back paws straightened out and is a skill we will use later when we teach the 2-on-2-off position.

- MEDIUM TABLE

  Put one end of the plank on the sixteen-inch-high table. Let your dog walk up the plank to the table, turn around, and then walk back down. Let your dog set the pace, but do not race him. Reward while your dog is moving to keep him focused and relaxed. Watch carefully for panic leaps. This tests his balance and basic understanding of the board. It also tells you that he knows where his paws are, particularly the rear. With most dogs you can also ask your dog to go halfway up the board, stop, and turn around. Again this simply encourages him to balance and adjust his paws on the board.

- HIGH TABLE

  Put one end of the plank on the twenty-four-inch-high table. Let your dog walk up the plank to the table, turn around, and then walk back down. Repeat multiple times and on both sides.

Teach the Entry

Once your dog can walk up the plank on a twenty-four-inch incline, it is time to teach him to find the dog walk entry on his own. Your goal is to get your dog to straighten his body *before* he gets on the plank. If your dog gets in the habit of straightening out once he is on the dog walk, he will eventually fall off. While many dogs simply leap to safety, at Mountain Freaks we teach angled approaches very early

> Heavy dogs can jiggle or move the plank at this height. Have a friend or your trainer hold the plank or secure it to the table.

and at a low height to minimize problems. Use the around-the-clock method (ten to two o'clock only) and begin with the plank on a sixteen-inch table. For clarity and safety, you also need to put wings on either side of the plank. Place the wings at the very end of the plank, making an entry "chute."

1. Set your dog in a sit about five feet from the end of the plank and move to the end of the wing chute. You should be facing the direction your dog is moving.

2. Recall your dog onto the plank. Reach inside the wing chute with the inside hand to lure the dog through and onto the plank.

3. Reward your dog once he has all four paws on the plank and is passing through the wing chute. Continue on with your dog to the table. Release your dog immediately from the table. Do not let him walk back down the plank.

Keep your hand low to help your dog maintain his balance.

Repeat for all the angles (ten to two o'clock) and then repeat entire drill with a twenty-four-inch table.

Across the Full Walk

Once your dog has completed all the plank work and can reliably keep his body straight, you can introduce the full dog walk. Remember, though, this is only an introduction. Let your dog practice running over the dog walk for two or three weeks. Since the goal is to teach your dog to stop at the end of the down ramp, you do not want your dog to practice running through the end. However, he needs to be confident and willing to drive across the entire obstacle before you ask for a new behavior.

For this exercise, set the middle board of the dog walk at about two feet. The incline should be similar to the one your dog worked with the high table. Reward by tossing a treat onto the floor in front of the plank as your dog exits the down ramp.

1. Place your dog on the down ramp of the dog walk about three feet from the end, at the edge of the yellow zone.

Trouble Shooting: If your dog is too heavy to pick up, place the table next to the dog walk. Have your dog jump on the table and then walk down the plank. Start with a sixteen-inch table and then switch to the twenty-four-inch table.

2. Release and let the dog gently walk off onto the floor. Toss the treat onto the floor.

3. Backchain in short increments, about one slat, with each repetition until your dog is walking or trotting over the entire dog walk.

Trouble Shooting: If your dog jumps off, repeat the exercise and be sure to stay even with your dog. If your dog looks back for you, he will loose his balance.

The Pause Table

Although it seems like the easiest obstacle to teach, the pause table can be deceptively hard. High-drive dogs do not like to stop the agility game. Why pause in the middle of a run? And many dogs like to surf the table (aka jump on the table and bounce right back off). Judges often put the table on course where the dog's stride is fully extended, challenging the team to prevent a quick surf or run by. Furthermore, since the table is the same size (only the height changes) for all divisions, it offers different challenges for dogs of different sizes. Large dogs must lie down immediately, since there is little room for maneuvering a big body in a thirty-six-inch square. Oversize breeds often land in a down with their paws drooping over the side. On the other hand, little dogs have plenty of room to bounce around, spin, or spend a few precious seconds investigating the surface before lying down, particularly if the surface is carpet or turf. Thus the table requires more than just a simple introduction.

High-drive dogs do not like to stop the agility game.

The pause table performance has three components. First the dog must get on the table and stop. Second the dog must do either a sit or a down. And finally the dog must wait for a five-second count. Although getting on the table sounds simple, your dog must be willing to collect his stride before leaping for the table. If he does not, the leap onto the table takes him right off the opposite side (aka surfing).

The second step requires that your dog understand a *Sit* and *Down* verbal command and be willing to down or sit. This can get tricky with a wet or mud table and downright nasty with a high-drive dog that knows a long wait is coming. Furthermore, even if you get your dog on the table and in a down, he still has to stay still while you move, the judge moves, and the count finishes! Many agility dogs get very good at listening to the judge's count and anticipate the *Go!* command.

VERBAL COMMANDS

We use two commands for the table. The *Table* command means "get on the table in a down position." The *Get Up* command means "get on the table in a sit position." If your dog knows the *Down* and *Sit* commands, then imbed the new command in the old for a few repetitions once you are working on the table. For example, do multiple reps with a *Table Down* and then alternately drop the *Down*. Mark and reward the down position when your dog responds to the *Table* command. A *Sit* command can be changed to *Get Up* with the same method. Before you work on the table, proof your dog's down and sit, making sure you can get a correct, timely response from your dog from a variety of positions, including a recall, from the side, and in motion.

You can also proof the wait on the flat, away from the obstacle. While proofing the down and sit, keep your dog in a position for different lengths of time. Count out loud to five, seven, ten, or even fifteen seconds. Move around while you count as a further proof of your dog's ability to wait for a formal release.

TRAIN THE TABLE

In order to train the collected stride to the table, we begin the table with a recall. Use an eight-inch or sixteen-inch table for the initial training. For large dogs, migrate to the higher table once the dog is reliably stopping on the low table. We also use a verbal mark such as *Yes!* for this exercise, since both hands are busy.

1. Put your dog in a sit about six feet from the table.

2. Move to the opposite side of the table from the dog and release the dog to the table by saying "Okay. Table."

3. As he leaps onto the table, guide his head down with a treat while you gently push down and back on his shoulders with the other hand. Mark and offer the reward as your dog's body flattens onto the table. Lean over the table slightly to encourage your dog to land and halt quickly. This also encourages big dogs to aim for the center of the table, not the far side.

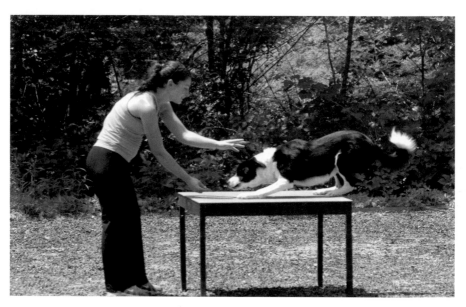

Guide the dog gently into a down as he leaps onto the table.

Ask for a down several times, then switch and ask for a sit. As the dog leaps onto the table, lift your right hand with the treat above the dog's nose. This encourages your dog to lift his head, which quite naturally drives his rear end down. For several sessions vary the down and sit positions and then begin to add distance to the table. Move your dog back in two-foot increments to a distance of about twenty feet. You should remain at the table, facing the dog.

As your dog leaps onto the table, lift the hand with the treat.

CHANGE THE HANDLER POSITION

Once your dog is able to halt in a sit or down on the table, you can begin to change your position relative to the table but put your dog closer to the table again, about six feet away. With each rep move back from the table in two-foot increments, to a distance of about fifteen feet. Continue to face the dog and always reward in position on the table. For example, if you asked for a down, reward a down. Do not let your dog sit and then reward. If he does sit first, gently lift his rear end into a stand before asking again for the down. For all these exercises vary the *Table* and *Get Up* commands and vary the wait time. Use a quick release, a five-second count, or a ten-second count. This keeps it interesting for the dog.

Once your dog can halt on the table with you at a distance, begin to move the dog back. As you move the dog away from the table, vary your position. For example, stand facing the direction your dog is moving. Stand close to the table for one rep, then move four feet away for the next.

Throughout the table exercises, watch also for focus from your dog. For the entire wait on the table, he should be watching you, not sniffing the table or selecting the next piece of equipment. Keep his focus on you. If you are losing his attention, shorten the distance and vary the wait time. Do a couple of quick releases off the table (less than a two-second wait) to keep his interest high. You can also put the table between two C-tunnels to make the table exercises more fun.

ADD HANDLER MOTION

The next step is to add handler motion. For all the initial training, you remained stationary and recalled the dog to the table. Now it is time to ask for the halt on the table even though you are moving. For all these exercises, mix up *Table* with *Get Up* and vary the wait time on the table. Reward frequently. It is also extremely important that the dog receive a clear release from the table.

Move with the Dog

The first variation is to move with your dog to the table. Put the dog ten to fifteen feet away from the table. Hold your dog in a restrained send, release him to the table by saying either "Go. Table." or "Go. Get Up," and move with him. Look at the table, not your dog, and do not point at the table. Let your dog offer the correct behavior. Reward and release.

Lateral Distance

Once you can move with your dog, begin adding lateral distance. It is helpful to place a bar, cone, or piece of tape on the ground to highlight the correct distance. Begin with three feet and work slowly (one foot at a time) away to a distance of fifteen or even twenty feet. For this exercise leave your dog in a stay, facing the table, and move directly to the right or left. Start the reps by standing about halfway between the dog and the table. Release the dog to the table and move forward. Stop when you are parallel to the middle of the table but still at the same lateral distance. Do not move to the table as you move forward. With success, move back incrementally until you are even with the dog.

Run By

The final exercise is to keep moving past the table. Even though you are still moving, your dog should stop and wait on the table. For the first reps, lead out halfway between the dog and table. With success, move back in two-foot increments until you can start level with or even behind your dog. Do the first run by at a slow pace and, with success, build up to a full run. Always reward on the table but return to your original position before releasing.

ADD A JUDGE

Another good exercise is to have a friend or training partner walk around in the vicinity of the table and count. Have your friend count aloud and put extra emphasis on *Go!* Do multiple reps to be sure your dog is not listening to the table count and anticipating the release. Make sure you wait an extra second or two after the *Go!* Do not habitually release your dog on the judge's *Go!*

Dog on table focusing on handler.

Judges frequently tell competitors during the course briefing that in agility *Go!* is a two-syllable word. The table count is typically, "Five and four and three and two and one and go." You must wait for the *o* in the *go* before you release your dog.

Advanced Target Work

A target is a training tool used to focus the dog's attention to a specific area. The actual target is an object, such as a plastic lid or tile, which is placed on the ground. It should be an object the dog will not try to pick up. The basics of target training were presented in chapter 5, Training ABCs. With the contacts, target training is expanded and the target behavior is refined to the end of the dog walk, seesaw, and A-frame. The actual target should be visible to the dog in the early training stages, although in the final stage the target is faded.

REVIEW TARGET WAIT

Before you begin working the target with the contacts, your dog must be reliably touching the target with the handler in a variety of positions and must be driving to the target. Repeat the exercises in chapter 5, Training ABCs, for target training as a quick refresher for you and your dog. You do not need to do every step, just a quick review.

Step 1: Introduce the Target

Step 2: Shape the Target Wait

Step 3: Run to the Target

Step 4: Shape the Wait

SHARPEN THE TARGET WAIT

A critical part of the 2-on-2-off position is the wait. Your dog must wait at the target until you release him. This also requires that the handler be rock-solid consistent with the release command. At this point in your training, you need to be sure your dog is waiting at the target until you release him. Remember to remain stationary through these exercises.

1. Hold the dog in a restrained send with the target ten feet in front, release your dog to the target.

2. Be patient! When your dog gets to the target, let him offer multiple touches. Mark the dog's *second* target wait. Toss the reward to the target.

3. Release the dog with *Okay*.

4. Send again to the target. Mark and reward the first target touch and then be patient. Since you did not release him, your dog should offer another target touch. Do not use another verbal command. Let your dog offer a behavior. Mark and reward the target touch. Release the dog with *Okay*.

Trouble Shooting: If your dog releases himself off the target, shorten the distance and try again.

Continue to vary the sequences with intermittent rewards for the target wait and a precise release off the target. The target is now officially a target wait.

At this point in the process, dogs that truly understand shaping will often offer different behaviors at the target. Remember you taught your dog to offer a different behavior or a variation of the behavior when the mark is withheld. This is the key component that makes shaping work. Your dog is thinking. When the handler does not immediately mark the target touch, many dogs will offer a second touch but others will offer a paw touch, scrape at the target, or a down on the target. Since you are shaping a wait (not a target tapping performance), you can accept multiple behaviors *so long as your dog stays at the target.* Do not mark behaviors that pull your dog off the target, and do not mark vocalizations such as whining or barking. Your dog may also simply offer a wait. Some dogs do stop and stand over the target. This is also correct, so mark and reward the stop/stand behavior but do not blur the line on where the dog stops. It must be at the target, not a few feet in front or to the side.

REWARD PLACEMENT

Before you continue your dog's target training, you need to be clear on how to reward the target wait. With body motion, reward placement becomes critical. Your dog will anticipate where you habitually place your rewards. As you begin to move, your dog will pull off the target. Thus rewarding at the target becomes critical. It is what keeps your dog at the target and waiting. You do not want a target wait and go. So at this point you must deliver the reward to the target, and your dog's anticipation of the reward placement will either raise or lower his success rate. It is the placement of the reward that is key.

Handler Ahead

Toss the reward back to the dog. He should receive it on the target or just in front of the target—no farther than a few inches.

Side-by-Side

Toss the reward away from your body so it lands on or just in front of the target. If the dog is wrapping around the target to get the reward, toss it slightly to the side of the target opposite you so that the dog has to turn away to get it.

Handler Behind

Toss the reward ahead at or just in front of the target. You want the dog to receive the reward from the front. If he practices turning around to receive his treat, he is practicing a move that will walk his back paws off the contact plank. If the dog insists on curling back to face you, go in and place the food on the target so he must move into position to get it.

It is also possible to use a toy at this stage. If your dog loves to play tug, get a long tug toy that allows you to hold with both hands while your dog tugs. To use a tug toy as the reward, mark the target wait and then step in and offer your dog the tug toy with one hand on each end of the toy. Stand directly in front of the dog. The dog should grab the center of the toy. It is important that your dog remain relatively stationary for this game, so keep the tug up and down directly over the target. Ask for the dog to release the toy and move back to your original spot before you release your dog from the target. This reinforces his understanding of wait and is an important skill used to proof contact performance.

ADD HANDLER MOTION

For all the initial target training the handler remains stationary. You send your dog to the target in front of you. Before you move the target performance on to the contact, you must proof your dog's target wait and release from a variety of positions and with motion. Do the following exercises over the course of a week or so and move on only when your dog is consistent at the lower exercise. Try them first in a quiet area so your dog can focus, and then try them in busy locations—in class or at a park—to test your dog's ability to focus exclusively on the target wait behavior.

We cannot emphasize enough the importance of a clear release from the target. You must formally release your dog from wait. This means with a single verbal command, like *Okay*. Since *Target* means "go there and wait," you should also continue to intermittently delay the mark to ensure that your dog understands that he must wait until released.

Move with the Dog

The first variation is to move with your dog to the target. Set the target ten to fifteen feet away. Hold your dog in a restrained send, release him to the target, and move with him. Look at the target, not your dog, and do not point at the target. Let your dog offer the correct behavior. Mark and reward the target wait. Release.

Lateral Distance

Once you can move with your dog, begin adding lateral distance. It is helpful to place a bar, cone, or piece of tape on the ground to highlight the correct distance. Begin with three feet and work slowly away (one foot at a time) to a distance of fifteen or even twenty feet. Stop when you are parallel to the target. Mark the stop and wait at the target and toss the treat sideways to the dog.

Recall

For this exercise put the dog in a wait ten feet from the target. Stand on the opposite side of the target, about five feet away, facing the direction your dog is going. Release your dog to the target. Remain stationary. Your dog should stop at the target. Mark his stop and toss the treat back at the target. If your dog moves over the target, remain neutral and give him a chance to back up and find the target. If he does not, retry but reduce the distances by half.

Run By

The third exercise is to keep moving past the target. Even though you are still moving, your dog should stop and offer a target wait. Start halfway between the dog and the target and work back to starting even with your dog. Do the first run by at a slow pace and, with success, build up to a full run. Always reward by tossing the treat back to the dog at the target.

ADVANCED DRILLS

There are a variety of exercises that you can work to sharpen your dog's target wait on the ground before you combine the target with the contacts. All of these will make the transition to the contact easier and smoother. They also give the handler lots of practice at timing the mark and formally releasing the dog. Furthermore, you can correct mistakes on the flat so your dog does not associate corrections with the equipment.

Release to Close

The first advanced exercise is to release your dog off the target to close. In all the previous drills, your dog was rewarded at the target. When the target was performed *incorrectly*, the dog received no mark, no reinforcement, no food, and no tug. However, as you start to sequence before and after the target, you do not want the absence of food or toy to communicate to your dog that he made a mistake. So it is important to teach him that another obstacle is also a reward.

Before you work the target into a sequence, your dog must be able to move off the target and receive a reward from you or from a different location without deteriorating his target performance.

1. Put your dog in a wait ten feet away from the target. Stand five feet in front of the target, facing the direction your dog is moving.

2. Release your dog to the target. With a deliberate target wait, move in and reward in position at the target. Remind the dog to wait and move back to your position when the dog stops. Then release with *Okay. Close.*

Trouble Shooting: If your dog delays leaving the target, make sure you are using a formal release and move forward a step or two to encourage your dog to come with you. Be patient and use a very desirable treat or toy for this drill. Remember: Your dog has had many lessons in receiving his reward on the target.

Once your dog is moving forward from the target into close, begin to vary the reward schedule. Reward a single target touch at the target or ask for a second target touch before releasing. Sometimes you can simply praise the dog in target position, then immediately release to close. Do not do this more than once for every four reps. Also make sure you are getting a deliberate target wait. Do not let your dog creep off the target.

With success you can begin to vary your handling position and add motion. For example, rather than stand on the opposite side of the target, you can move laterally or you can run by the target. With each rep, release after a deliberate target wait and call your dog to *Close.*

Release to Toy/Treat

The next exercise is to place a treat or toy on the floor five feet in front of the target. This will draw your dog's attention away from the target.

1. Put your dog in a wait ten feet away from the target. Put a toy/treat on the floor five feet in front of the target. Stand next to the toy/treat to keep your dog from getting it until you release him from the target.

2. Release your dog to the target. With a deliberate target wait, go in and reward your dog in the stopped position and then release him to the toy/treat.

> **Trouble Shooting:** If your dog goes past the target but does not go for the treat, be patient. Give him a chance to offer the correct behavior. Mark the target wait and reward at the target. Repeat the exercise.

> **Trouble Shooting:** If your dog blasts right over the target, step on the toy/treat and collect the dog. Try again with the dog closer to the target and the treat farther away.

With success, vary the distance to the target and then move farther from the toy/treat.

Target and Go

Another game that dogs enjoy reinforces the "target and go" concept. This exercise also helps handlers develop an eye for correct performance done in motion. It uses two tunnels and the target. Racing through a tunnel encourages your dog to extend his stride. In addition to adding an obstacle as a reward, this exercise allows him to practice locating the target with an extended stride.

Set up two C-shaped tunnels approximately thirty feet apart with the target on the ground between them. Put the target about ten feet away from one of the tunnel entrances. For this exercise your dog's reward is to continue the sequence.

1. Hold your dog in a restrained send and release to the tunnel with the target. Always start with a tunnel to get speed to the target and move with your dog.

2. With a deliberate target wait, mark and then immediately release him to the second tunnel. Reward at the tunnel exit.

3. On the second rep, ask for a longer target wait and then go in to reward in the stopped position before you release the dog to the tunnel.

The second phase of this drill is to change the ratio of tunnel-to-food/toy rewards. What you did first was fifty/fifty—once the dog was rewarded with the tunnel, once he was rewarded with food/toy. The second rep rewarded a prolonged target wait. Now try doing three repetitions of the tunnel to target. Reward the dog with a tunnel on the first two correct target waits, and on the third target wait reward with food/toy. When he is successful with this reward schedule, change it! For example, do four repetitions of tunnel to target. Reward the first target wait with a tunnel, the second target wait with food/toy, the third target with a tunnel, and the last target with food/toy. Then try for a total of five tunnel-to-target wait reps, only giving your dog food/toy on the third and fifth repetitions. We like to build the dogs up to hitting the target perfectly at least six or seven times before getting a food or toy reward. At that point we know the dog has excellent commitment to the target and will reliably drive to it in a variety of circumstances. It is important to train the target behavior well enough so that it does not break down in the absence of food or a toy.

Jump to Target

Once your dog can reliably target wait in a tunnel sequence, we like to add in a single jump ahead of the target. Using another piece of equipment continues to strengthen the dog's commitment to the target and allows him to practice striding to the target. Remember to stop at the target; your dog must shorten or collect his stride. This is made more difficult by the incline on the down ramp of the dog walk and even worse on the steep A-frame. We teach the dog how to control his stride length—in order to stop comfortably and safely at the target—by having the dog take a jump and then target. Landing off the jump and taking one stride to reach the target require your dog to control his stride and be willing to adjust it to halt at the target. Use food when you initially teach this exercise. Only switch to a toy once the dog is performing the exercise perfectly.

For this exercise use a single wingless jump set at a low height, such as half your dog's normal height. Ideally your dog should land off the jump, take one stride to the target, and then stop to grab his food reward. This is a physically challenging exercise. Initially you may find that your dog falls to the side or goes forward over the target. Do not progress in this exercise until he is physically strong and coordinated enough to come to a stop after taking one stride to the target.

1. Put your dog one dog length from the jump and put the target two dog lengths away on the opposite side. Stand slightly in front of the target with your feet facing the direction your dog is moving.

2. Release your dog over the jump to the target. Mark and reward a target wait. Your reward should be tossed down to the dog, landing on or just in front of the touch board. Stay consistent with your reward placement.

With each successful rep move your dog back one dog length and repeat. Keep moving back to a distance of fifteen to twenty feet. To ensure success you must also move the target out after every few reps. This allows your dog to land comfortably and still hit the target as his stride extends with the increased distance to the jump.

Two-On-Two-Off Wait

The next phase changes the general wait at the target behavior into a full 2-on-2-off wait. Up until now your dog simply waited at the target to be released. Now we are going to shape that wait into a specific position: two paws on the ground and two paws on the plank.

The 2-on-2-off position must be precise.

The 2-on-2-off position must be precise. It is not one foot on and three off. It is not three on and one off. It is not done on an angle off the side of the plank. And it is a precise stop. The dog cannot skid to a stop off the plank and then back onto the plank. Nor can the dog stop in a 2-on-2-off position and then release himself. Remember that with shaping, the end result—the final desired behavior—must be concrete. It cannot be general, which is why we do not use a halt with four paws on the plank. If you try to get your dog to stop on the plank, you must be absolutely precise about where the stop is. This gets more and more difficult as the dog speeds up and the handler is in a variety of positions. It is also much harder on the dog's shoulders to stop with four paws on the A-frame. Stopping with two paws on the ground is concrete and easy for the handler to visualize. The dog can also feel the surface difference beneath his paws. It has no variation. And it is the same behavior across all three contacts.

SHAPE THE 2-ON-2-OFF POSITION

The goal is to get your dog to stop at the target in a 2-on-2-off position and wait. At this point in the process, you are no longer marking a target wait. You are marking a specific position and a wait. The target at the end of the plank is now just a reminder. It encourages your dog to focus on the obstacle and the behavior versus the handler, which eventually allows the handler to move on a line independent to the dog's.

We typically do the 2-on-2-off training with the dog walk planks. For the first exercise set the middle plank flat on the ground and send your dog onto it from the side (i.e., on a perpendicular line). This gives your dog a wider area to place his back paws while he locates the target and you shape a 2-on-2-off position (front paws on the ground, rear paws on the plank). The middle plank is easier to work with since it does not have slats.

Send your dog onto the plank from the side.

1. Place the target six to twelve inches away from the *middle* of the plank, far enough out to get the dog's front paws and shoulders off the plank. Sit or kneel on the floor next to your dog on the opposite side of the plank from the target. This position has two advantages. First, you are sending your dog to the target, and second, being behind the target (vs ahead) encourages him to stop.

2. With your hand in his collar, release your dog and let him offer target. Mark and reward any target wait where the dog puts his front paws on the floor and keeps his rear paws on the plank. Be patient and consistent with the criteria. You are shaping a new behavior.

3. Release your dog from the 2-on-2-off position.

After several reps, switch to a restrained send. Mark and reward any target wait where the dog assumes and holds a 2-on-2-off position. Be patient with your mark. You want your dog to understand that this is a wait.

With success, stand up and then increase the distance from the plank in small increments until he can find 2-on-2-off from ten or fifteen feet. You should remain next to the plank and stationary. Vary the wait at the target. At this point in your training, you can also reward the target wait with a tug in place.

SHARPEN THE 2-ON-2-OFF POSITION

When your dog can reliably find the 2-on-2-off position from a distance to the long side of the plank, it is time to work the dog the length of the plank. Although the plank is still flat on the ground, this requires more precision from the dog with regard to body position and requires that the dog understands the changed criteria. *Target wait* means more than just touch the target with a nose or paw. It now means wait in a 2-on-2-off position at the end of the plank.

For the first few sessions, place a wing at the end of the plank on the opposite side from the handler. The wing acts as a guide, which keeps the dog's body straight and his paws on the plank as he hops on.

1. Hop your dog onto the plank just above the yellow zone. Using a restrained send, ask for *Target*, which now means "move to the 2-on-2-off position and wait." Mark and reward the wait, which must be in a 2-on-2-off position.

Trouble Shooting: If your dog jumps off the plank or touches the target and releases, simply guide him back and retry without the restrained send.

2. Backchain the length of the plank in one-foot increments until the dog is consistently driving forward and stopping in a 2-on-2-off position at the end of the plank.

Trouble Shooting: If your dog moves before you release him, guide him back to the plank and have him hop on just above the yellow zone. Ask again for a target wait (aka 2-on-2-off position) and reward verbally. Repeat the exercise that caused the error. If he breaks again, change the criteria, use less motion, or stay closer and resume in smaller increments.

After you have backchained the length of the plank, vary your position and add motion. Stand halfway down the plank facing the direction the dog is moving and move with your dog to the target. Or move a few feet ahead of the plank and recall your dog to the target. Use a variety of positions: send, recall, run by, and lateral distance. You can also reward your dog's wait with a game of tug. Remain stationary and tug up and down directly over the target.

You can also reward a 2-on-2-off wait with a tug in place.

You can also switch sides before releasing your dog. At this point you are training the 2-on-2-off position as a wait. Your dog cannot move until you release him, regardless of where you are. If you pass the dog, he should stop. If you cross in front of him, he should remain in place. If you move laterally left or right, he should stay put.

RAISE THE PLANK

Once your dog is consistently offering a 2-on-2-off wait on the flat plank, it is time to add a slight incline. Put the up or down plank of the dog walk on the sixteen-inch table and use two wings to keep the dog straight as he exits. Place a visible target at the end of the plank. Your goal is to have your dog drive down the plank and then stop in a 2-on-2-off position. It is also absolutely critical that the dog wait until he is released, regardless of the handler's position or motion. Remember to work both the right and left sides.

1. Hop your dog onto the plank just above the wing.

2. Release to the target. Mark the 2-on-2-off wait, reward, and release.

3. Put the dog back at the same spot on the plank and hold him in a restrained send with the inside hand. Release the dog to the target. Mark the 2-on-2-off wait, reward, and then release.

After several successful reps, begin backchaining to the table. Move your dog back in short, one-foot increments. Continue to use a restrained send and move with your dog to the end of the plank. Mark the 2-on-2-off wait and vary the duration of the wait. Do not rush to reward and release. You can also delay the mark on some reps to be sure your dog will wait.

At this point in the training, we like to switch from a click to a verbal mark, such as *Yes!* Using a verbal mark allows you to mark from a distance and in the ring once you are trialing.

ADD HANDLER MOTION

Once your dog is consistently offering a 2-on-2-off wait, vary your position and add motion. Stand halfway down the plank facing the direction the dog is moving and move with your dog to the target. Or move a few feet ahead of the plank and recall your dog to the target from the table. You can also increase the lateral distance in short increments, up to about six feet. Use a variety of positions: send, recall, run by, and lateral distance. You can also switch sides before releasing your dog. At this point you are again proofing the 2-on-2-off position as a wait. Your dog cannot move until you release him, regardless of where you are. If you pass the dog, he should stop. If you cross in front of him, he should remain in place. If you move laterally left or right, he should stay put. At this point we also remove the wing chute.

The Dog Walk

After you have worked the dog-walk plank on an incline, you can work both the dog walk and A-frame exercises concurrently. Although the dog walk is presented first, you do not have to complete the dog walk training before you move to the A-frame or seesaw. In fact we like to keep the dogs engaged and interested by working all the contacts in short sessions a few times a week.

BACKCHAIN THE DOG WALK

After your dog can hold a 2-on-2-off wait at the end of an inclined plank regardless of the handler's motion and position, it is time to move to the full dog walk. Set the dog walk at twenty-four inches, as measured on the middle plank of the dog walk. Use a visible target.

1. Have the dog hop onto the down plank just above the yellow zone.

2. Use a restrained send. Mark the 2-on-2-off wait, reward, and then release.

3. Backchain the dog walk. Move your dog back in short, one-foot increments across the down ramp, middle plank, and then the up ramp. Once you reach the end of the up ramp, have a friend hold your dog in a restrained send so you can remain at the edge of the yellow zone. This minimizes your motion as your dog practices the 2-on-2-off wait from a distance and with more speed.

> **Trouble Shooting:** If your dog stops above the target, remain neutral and let him offer a target wait. Reward immediately and then repeat the exercise. If he stops above the 2-on-2-off position and remains stuck, go in and gently guide him by the collar to the 2-on-2-off position. Praise verbally and then have him hop on above the yellow zone and find 2-on-2-off wait on his own. Praise verbally and then repeat the exercise.

Once your dog is working across the entire dog walk, raise the dog walk in one-foot increments. With each height change, backchain the entire dog walk again. For large dogs you can place the twenty-four-inch table next to the dog walk and lift your dog onto the dog walk from the table. Thus the lift is never more than two feet.

This is also where you should add a verbal command for the obstacle. At Mountain Freaks we prefer *Walk* since it is a short, distinct sound. We do not use *Dog Walk*. The extra word is not necessary.

After your dog is working on a full-length, full-height dog walk, it is time to proof the 2-on-2-off wait, put the dog-walk performance into a short sequence, and then add handler motion. It is important to proof the 2-on-2-off wait fully before putting the dog walk into a sequence. With the obstacle in a sequence, too many things can go wrong, which makes it harder to correct the 2-on-2-off wait.

PROOF THE 2-ON-2-OFF WAIT

The first step in the proofing process is to repeat the backchain with a visible toy. Use a full-height dog walk and place a toy on the ground in front of the down plank. The toy encourages your dog to keep his head down and increases his desire to drive off the plank. Your goal is to get your dog to drive forward down the ramp but still hold the 2-on-2-off wait.

1. Hold your dog in a restrained send at the top of the yellow zone and release to the target.

> **Trouble Shooting:** If your dog goes directly to the toy, try again with the toy twice as far away. If your dog bypasses the 2-on-2-off wait again, have a training partner put a foot on the toy to prevent the dog from receiving his reward until released.

2. Mark when your dog halts at the target. Reward in position with food and then immediately release your dog to the toy.

3. Backchain the entire down walk. As you move up the plank, make sure that you move back to your starting position after you reward with food but prior to releasing your dog to the toy. You should also vary the wait time at the target.

At this point we like to proof the dog-walk performance with a variety of drills. Use the following in order and have a friend hold the dog in a restrained send at the top of the down ramp. Stand at the end of the down plank.

- Put the toy on a slight angle but on same side as the handler. Look for your dog to stop in a 2-on-2-off wait. With this drill we want the dog to come off the plank straight and at the end. The dog should not exit off the side. With success, begin to deepen the angle, up to about forty-five degrees.

- Put the toy on an angle on the opposite side of the handler. Again we are looking for the dog to stop in a 2-on-2-off wait and exit off the plank straight. With success, begin to deepen the angle, up to about forty-five degrees.

- Put a low jump after the dog walk, about fifteen feet away. Put the toy at the opposite side of the jump and release the dog over the jump to the toy after rewarding the target wait in position. We are looking for the dog to stop in a 2-on-2-off wait even though the toy is farther away, and we are asking for a different performance after the release.

- Put a C-tunnel after the dog walk. After you step in and reward the target wait in position, release the dog from the target into the tunnel. We are looking for the dog to stop in a 2-on-2-off wait, even with the enticement of a tunnel, and the desire to extend his stride on the way to the tunnel.

SHORT SEQUENCES

With the dog proofed on a 2-on-2-off wait, it is time for the handler to begin to interface with dog. The exercise we use has a wing-jump set perpendicular to the dog walk and at the edge of the yellow zone. Set the bar at a relatively low height. For the first few reps, send your dog over the jump and ask him to hop on the dog walk after he lands. You should remain on the takeoff side of the jump and be moving past the bottom of the plank as your dog hops on. Mark the 2-on-2-off wait and reward the dog with a treat tossed back at the target. There are multiple goals from this exercise. First, your dog gets to practice the 2-on-2-off wait with a little bit of speed and from another obstacle. Second, the handler can work from different positions, including a rear cross on the jump and a front cross on the plank. And finally, this is where we begin to shrink the target. Reduce the size of your target by about 50 percent.

Once the dog understands how to hop onto the dog walk from the side, we like to proof the dog with more speed and with different handler positions. Remember to work both the left and right sides.

- Change the configuration to two wing jumps, one on either side of the dog walk, and a C-tunnel. This configuration allows

The jump, tunnel, dog walk configuration allows you to get multiple 2-on-2-off waits in one sequence.

you to move with the dog through a variety of sequences and get multiple 2-on-2-off waits. For example, send the dog over the jump, onto the dog walk, release to the tunnel, and then send over the opposite jump and back onto the dog walk. For all of these exercises, move with your dog but vary your handling to include both the left and right sides, front crosses, and rear crosses.

- Change your position and stand behind the jump. Hold the dog in a restrained send about halfway up the down ramp and release to the target. Mark the 2-on-2-off wait and then recall your dog back over the jump. Immediately ask him to hop onto the dog walk and repeat the 2-on-2-off wait. Remember to toss the reward at or slightly ahead of the target.

- Send your dog to the jump with lateral distance. By this time your dog should understand how to hop onto the dog walk and offer a 2-on-2-off wait. Stand to the side, increasing the lateral distance with each rep, and then send your dog over the jump and onto the dog walk. Maintain your lateral distance as your dog reaches the target. With this drill we also begin to release the dog on an angle. Since you are in front or to the side of the dog for these exercises, toss the treat back to the dog at the target.

ADD HANDLER MOTION

When your dog is consistent with his 2-on-2-off wait with you in a variety of positions, it is time to add motion. With the handler in motion, a dog must truly understand the concept of wait. All of these exercises are done on the full-height dog walk. Reward your dog frequently with food or a tug game, but always use a clear release word. Do the following exercises over the course of a week or so and move on only when your dog is consistent at the previous exercises.

Recall

The first variation is to recall your dog over the dog walk. For this exercise put the dog in a wait five feet from the up ramp. Stand at the end of the down ramp, facing the direction your dog is going. Release your dog and reward the 2-on-2-off wait.

Lateral Distance

You can also add lateral distance. It is helpful to place a bar, cone, or piece of tape on the ground to highlight the correct distance. Begin with three feet and work slowly out and away to a distance of ten or even fifteen feet. Stop when you are even with or just beyond the end of the plank.

Restrained Send

For this exercise, hold your dog in a restrained send at the end of the dog walk. Release him to the target and run with him. Mark the 2-on-2-off wait. If you fall behind, walk in and reward your dog at the target but return to your original spot before releasing the dog.

Run By

The final exercise is to keep moving past the target. Even though you are still moving, your dog should do a 2-on-2-off wait. Start at the top of the down ramp and work back to starting even with your dog. Do the first run by at a slow pace and, with success, build up to a full run. Always reward by tossing or dropping the treat at the target.

UP ZONE

At Mountain Freaks we do not teach an up-zone behavior unless the dog's natural stride can easily and consistently carry it over the entire forty-two-inch zone. This is unusual. For the dogs with extremely large strides, we teach a paw touch on a touch board.

The A-Frame

Once your dog can hold a 2-on-2-off wait at the end of an inclined plank regardless of the handler's motion and position, you can begin to work on the A-frame.

BACKCHAIN THE A-FRAME

Set the A-frame at a very low height, about three feet at the apex.

1. Put the dog on the down ramp of the A-frame just above the yellow zone with a visible target.

2. Use a restrained send. Mark the 2-on-2-off wait, reward, and then release.

3. Backchain the A-frame. Move your dog back in short one-foot increments. Once you reach the top, have a friend hold your dog in a restrained send so you can remain at the edge of the yellow zone. This minimizes your motion as your dog practices the 2-on-2-off wait from a distance and with more speed.

Trouble Shooting: If your dog stops above the target, remain neutral and let him offer a target wait. Reward immediately and then repeat the exercise. If he stops above the 2-on-2-off position and remains stuck, go in and gently guide him by the collar to the 2-on-2-off position. Praise verbally and then have him hop on above the yellow zone and find the 2-on-2-off wait on his own. Praise verbally and then repeat the exercise.

Once your dog is working across the entire A-frame, raise the apex in six-inch increments. With each height change, backchain the entire A-frame again but work the up ramp in one step. As you raise the A-frame, many dogs cannot get enough momentum to easily clear the top as the incline increases.

This is also where you should add a verbal command for the obstacle. Common choices are *Frame, Climb,* or *Scramble.* At Mountain Freaks we use *Frame,* because it is a distinct sound.

Momentum and drive send even small dogs over the top of the A-frame with ease.

(Photo courtesy of Joe Canova)

After your dog is working on a full-height A-frame, it is time to proof the target wait, put the A-frame performance into a short sequence, and then add handler motion. It is important to proof the 2-on-2-off wait fully before putting the A-frame into a sequence. The height and angle of the A-frame make the 2-on-2-off wait difficult, particularly for long-backed dogs.

Repeat all the drills and exercises used to proof and train the dog walk.

- Proof the 2-on-2-off wait

- Short sequences

- When using an A-frame in this drill, set the A-frame to full height but place the jumps halfway through the yellow zone. This gives the dog room to land the jump and get on the A-frame with it at a reasonable height.

- Add handler motion

Seesaw

The seesaw or teeter-totter is one of the more difficult obstacles to teach. Many dogs do not like the sensation of a plank falling beneath their paws. It is not uncommon for dogs to refuse the seesaw, jump off, or leap frantically through the pivot point. In order for dogs to be comfortable with the seesaw, we use a slow, steady progression that allows them to get used to the motion of the plank without inducing panic.

Constructed of one twelve-foot wood or metal plank, the seesaw is typically twelve inches wide with a pivot point that is twenty-four to twenty-seven inches high. With a twenty-four-inch-high pivot point, the high end of the seesaw is about four feet, six inches. The seesaw has a contact or yellow zone that is typically thirty-six inches long but has no slats. In all the registries the dog must put at least one foot in the contact zone on both ends of the plank and more than one foot for safety. Furthermore the dog must still be in contact with the seesaw plank when it hits the ground. All the registries consider a "seesaw fly off" an eliminating fault, which is when the dog leaps off the plank before it touches the ground.

For dogs under fifteen pounds, we teach the dog to stop with all four paws on the seesaw. This position is safer. With lightweight dogs the plank can bounce back up as the dog halts in a 2-on-2-off position, which takes half the dog's weight off the seesaw. Small dogs can

With a well-timed release, the handler can send the dog on to the next obstacle as the seesaw hits the ground.

actually get lifted back up or hit by the seesaw plank. For these dogs we place the target at the very end of the plank.

For the following exercises, set the seesaw to about fourteen inches at the pivot point and place the up side of the seesaw on a sixteen-inch table. In this configuration the seesaw is inclined down with a two- to three-inch rise off the floor.

PULL DOWN THE PLANK

Before the dogs get on the plank, we like to have them first pull or push the plank down. This gives the dog control over the plank's motion. Sit or kneel on the floor at the end of the seesaw and let your dog step on the plank. Mark and reward your dog for pushing the plank to the floor with his front paws. Your goal is to get your dog to push or even slam the plank onto the floor. Reward when your dog has two paws on the plank. He does not need to get on the plank.

INCLINE THE PLANK DOWN

The next step is to let the dog walk the length of the seesaw plank from the table. As he gets to the end, his weight will naturally push the plank down a few inches. It is important to use a two- or three-inch drop and to backchain to the table. You can also place wings on either side of the end of the plank to keep your dog moving straight. Place the target at the end of the seesaw and remember to work both the left and right sides.

1. Have your dog hop onto the seesaw from just above the yellow zone.

2. Let him offer a 2-on-2-off position, or 4-on for small dogs. Mark, reward, and release.

3. Backchain in one-foot increments the length of the plank. For this exercise you should be moving with your dog to the end of the plank.

PROOF THE 2-ON-2-OFF WAIT

Once your dog is consistently offering a 2-on-2-off wait or 4-on wait on the down plank, add handler motion. You are still using the see-saw inclined slightly off the table. Do the following exercises over the course of a week or so. Reward frequently with food or a tug game, but always use a clear release word.

Restrained Send

For this exercise hold your dog in a restrained send on the table. Release him down the inclined plank to the target. Remain stationary. Mark the 2-on-2-off wait. Walk in and reward, but then return to your original spot. Release the dog once you are back to the table.

Run By

The opposite exercise is to move past the target. Even though you are still moving, your dog should do a 2-on-2-off wait. Do the first run by at a slow pace and, with success, build up to a full run. Always reward by tossing the treat back to the target.

Lateral Distance

You can also add lateral distance. It is helpful to place a bar, cone, or piece of tape on the ground to highlight the correct distance. Begin with two feet and work slowly out and away to a distance of ten or even fifteen feet. Stop when you are even with or just beyond the end of the plank.

Recall

The final variation is to recall your dog over the seesaw. For this exercise put the dog in a wait on the table. Stand at the end of the plank, facing the direction your dog is going. Release your dog and reward the 2-on-2-off wait.

Recall your dog over the seesaw inclined down from the table.

LEVEL PLANK

The next step is to work the dog on a level seesaw. Raise the pivot point of the seesaw to sixteen inches and place the up side of the plank on the sixteen-inch table. In this configuration the seesaw plank is level and your dog is riding the plank down from a height of sixteen inches. Repeat the backchain and proof drills.

INCLINE THE PLANK UP

When the dog is comfortable on a sixteen-inch-high level seesaw, we begin letting the dog walk up an incline and then ride the plank down. This is confusing to many dogs. Walking up is counterintuitive to then riding down. However, after the last two drills, your dog should understand how to ride the plank down and his adjustment should be fairly quick. For this exercise remove the table and lower the seesaw pivot to about twelve inches. Repeat the backchain and proof drills.

In six-inch increments, work the seesaw to full height, always doing the backchain before the 2-on-2-off proof drills.

This is also where you should add a verbal command for the obstacle. Common choices are *Seesaw, Teeter, Tip-It,* or simply *Saw.* At Mountain Freaks we use *Seesaw,* since it avoids the *t* sound and is distinct.

Fade the Target

Once the dog is working the obstacles in short sequences, we begin to fade the target on the down ramp. This is a relatively quick process. After all the backchains and proofing work, your dog understands a 2-on-2-off wait and is now focused on the wait, not the target. At the end of the proofing, it merely exists as a visual reminder to your dog to wait. Furthermore, you have been rewarding with a treat tossed at the target for several weeks, so your dog is already focused on your hand for the reward. Thus the first step is to reward the dog from your hand and not toss the reward at the target. This encourages your dog to stay connected to you and stay alert for a release. The second step is to remove the target. During your sequence work put the target on two of the three contacts and alternate the contacts that have the target. We also alternate the rewards. This includes your verbal praise. Reward the first contact with food by walking in and feeding from the hand closest to the dog. For the second and third contacts in a sequence, verbally mark and then immediately release. On the next sequence verbally mark the first and second and reward the third with food. Continue to alternate and mix up your reward schedule.

If your dog begins to stop on the contact, for a few sequences put the smaller target back out as a reminder to your dog to find the 2-on-2-off position.

If your dog begins to creep down the contact to the 2-on-2-off position, let him run over the entire obstacle, similar to the introduction exercise, releasing him as soon as his front paws are on the ground. Loosen him up and let him run. Then backchain the restrained sends with a visible target. Your goal is to increase his drive and rebalance the 2-on-2-off wait. You should also be careful when and where you say *Target*. If you say the command early (i.e., before your dog hits the yellow zone), he may think you are asking him to stop above the 2-on-2-off position. Time your verbal command to when your dog is in the yellow zone, or say nothing at all. Your dog should understand that a 2-on-2-off wait is required at the end of every down plank.

CHAPTER 10

Weave Pole Introduction

Spectators love to watch dogs weave. A fast-weaving dog elicits instant clapping and cheering. However, the weave poles are also considered one of the more challenging obstacles for dogs to learn and are one of the most frequently faulted obstacles on an agility course, regardless of the level.

Most registries use six poles at the beginning level, with the more advanced levels using ten or twelve poles. The weave poles must be attached to a solid base, either metal or wood, and are spaced between twenty-one and twenty-four inches apart. Poles are almost always constructed of half-inch or three-quarter-inch PVC pipe and are generally forty-two inches high.

At Mountain Freaks we do not believe weave poles are difficult to teach, but they are one of the most time-consuming obstacles on which to achieve a consistent performance. To this end we train weave poles in a specific, step-by-step method that eliminates problems. Our goal is to train weaves that are accurate and fast under all conditions. Our dogs literally hunt for the weaves, and they weave efficiently regardless of where the handler is or where the handler moves. Independent-weave pole competency is based on training not handling. A rock-solid foundation gives the dog the ability to find the weave pole entry from any location and to stay in the poles regardless of distractions.

Weave poles are unique in that the dog must learn to ignore his handler's motion. A consistent agility dog has a weave pole performance that is truly independent. This is the opposite of groundwork training, which means the weave poles must be put into sequences very carefully. Weave poles are also age restricted. The decision to begin weaving depends on the breed and the individual dog's maturity. As a general rule we do not teach weave poles until a dog is at least eight months old, and frequently we wait until the dog is a year old. Weaving is strenuous and requires considerable mental focus. You can lure dogs younger than eight months old through and around the poles with a toy or treat to get them accustomed to the feel of the metal base and to let them become familiar with crossing back and forth between poles. We like to play tug around and between the poles so that our young dogs get used to the base and to bumping into the poles. Once your dog is old enough, you can begin training the weave poles.

Weave pole training is a process. It requires discipline from the handler to proceed slowly and methodically through the steps so the dog learns to weave correctly from the beginning. Like the dog walk, weave poles have several distinct components to the performance: entry, weaving, and exit. Your dog must be proficient at all three. The entry is defined as the space between poles 1 and 2. Regardless of where you are or how your dog approaches the weaves, he must enter the weaves between poles 1 and 2 and from right to left (assuming the poles are directly ahead). He must then weave through all the poles. The exit is between the last two poles (either 5 and 6 or 11 and 12). If he wove correctly, your dog will exit the weave poles moving from right to left also.

Since weave poles are mentally and physically challenging, your dog should be well rested and interested in working. Give him quiet time before and after every training session. Train weave poles early in your class or training session so your dog is hungry and interested in attention. Train in five- to ten-minute sessions and work in an area without distractions.

Methods and Styles

There are a variety of methods used to train weave poles and a variety of weaving styles that dogs develop.

After decades of agility training, a number of methods have evolved to teach weave poles. All are successful and can be used with most dogs. Common methods include 2-by-2, wires, weave-a-matic, and channel. For the 2-by-2 method, the dog is introduced to the poles in sets of two. The weave behavior is shaped slowly—two weave poles at a time—until the dog is weaving six or twelve poles. The wire method uses curved wires around a straight set of weaves, thereby creating a curved channel. The curves force the dog to weave between poles. One of the most common methods is the weave-a-matic, which slants the poles right and left off the base. Thus the dog is presented with a V-channel down the center. With many repetitions the V is gradually closed and the dog learns to weave between straight poles. Like the weave-a-matic, the channel method also opens the poles, but side to side rather than on a slant. As the dog becomes proficient at weaving, this allows the dog to consistently see straight poles while the opening or channel down the middle of the poles is closed.

Regardless of the equipment used to teach the weaves, the ultimate goal is to get the dog to weave consistently and with speed. Both are dependent to a certain extent on the striding in the weaves, which is in turn dependent on the dog's size and structure. Very small dogs, such as Chihuahuas, Japanese Chins, or Pomeranians, can often trot or walk between the poles. Small and medium-size dogs frequently hop back and forth through the weaves. In order to hop the dog places two feet on each side of the alternate weave poles and literally hops in and out.

When a dog hops the poles, he puts both front feet on the same side of the pole.

This is an easy style for many dogs to adopt and is frequently seen with poodles, shelties, Cavaliers, and many of the terriers. Hopping requires perfect timing but allows the dogs to be very consistent.

The most common striding for large dogs in the weaves is single stride. To single stride the poles, the dog places one leg on either side of the weave poles. Viewed from the front, the dog appears to swim through the poles.

Single striding requires the dog's front legs to be long enough to reach pole to pole, and the dog must learn to drive from behind. Large, heavy dogs that learn to single stride often drive forward enough to actually push the weave aside as they move down the center.

When a dog single strides the weaves, he puts one front foot on either side of the poles.

Large, heavy dogs can push open weave poles when they single stride.

At Mountain Freaks we use the channel method and work with individual handlers to determine which style works best for their dog. As a general rule shoulder height can be used to determine striding style. Dogs below eighteen inches at the shoulder typically hop. Dogs over eighteen inches typically single stride. However, the dog will do whatever stride naturally works better for him. We do not try to change that. Either style can be fast and accurate. Smaller dogs, under eighteen inches, usually prefer to hop, and larger dogs usually prefer to single stride. What is important is consistency. The dog must hop or single stride through all the poles. Dogs that alternate their footwork in the poles are less accurate and are prone to pulling out or missing poles.

Handlers also need a good eye to analyze their dog's striding. We recommend having a training partner watch, or better yet videotape, your dog in the poles. Even during the introduction phase, if the dog is alternating between hopping and single striding, we like to induce the dog to stick to single stride. Our best method for this correction is to use the weave-a-matics with a fifteen-degree angle, which encourages the dog to single stride. This works even if the dog was initially trained with other methods. It is for this reason that we do not start small dogs on the weave-a-matics. At Mountain Freaks smaller dogs, those under eighteen inches, start on channel weaves. Larger dogs can and do learn to single stride with any type of weave poles.

Mark your channel weaves slide out in inches. This allows you to set the poles at the same distance quickly and without constantly guessing. It also lets you keep track of your dog's performance, which is particularly important in a class situation. You can easily remind your instructor that your dog is currently weaving at four inches or two inches. Week to week, this makes your training consistent.

Introduce the Poles

Before you ask your dog to move down the center of the weave poles, let him wander around them. Some dogs view the weaves as a fence and are reluctant to pass through them. You should not mark a perpendicular pass through the weaves, but you can lure your dog through with a treat. Have a dog that loves the weaves go through the channel several times first. Let your dog watch the other dog get rewarded for going through the weave channel. Play tug around and through the weaves to get your dog accustomed to the metal base and the rigidity of the poles.

For the introduction use a set of six poles with the channel open about six inches. If you are on weave-a-matics, the poles should be open about ninety degrees.

1. Put the dog about ten feet from the first pole and have a friend or instructor hold him in a restrained recall.

2. Move to the end of the poles.

3. Release the dog and mark the entry with a verbal marker. We like to use a brisk *Yes!* Reward as the dog exits past pole 6. Hold the treat low so your dog keeps his head down.

> **Trouble Shooting:** If your dog refuses to enter the poles or skips out in the middle, give a neutral response (look away for a brief moment) and then try again. Move to the center between poles 3 and 4 and call the dog to you. With success, move back one pole at a time until the dog runs freely through all six poles.

> **Trouble Shooting:** If your dog is slow in the poles, help build drive by walking backward as your dog exits pole 6. You can also add a short, straight tunnel before the poles to add drive into the poles.

Work on the weave introduction for a week or two, doing several reps in each training session. Remember to have your dog holder release the dog from both the left and right. Keep the dog on a straight line to the poles.

Once your dog is moving briskly through the open weaves, fade the restrained recall and have your dog wait on his own. You should continue to face the dog and recall him through the weaves. Your goal is to have your dog move deliberately and speedily through the six weave poles.

This is also where you should add a verbal command. Common choices are *Weave, Wiggle*, or *Poles*.

Add Handler Motion

With a dog that will offer a pass through six poles, you can begin to add handler motion. Your goal is to walk with your dog for the length of six poles and to build drive through the poles. You also want drive as you turn in and recall the dog to you. This phase generally goes very quickly, assuming you are training every day. Remember to work the left and right sides. This first phase also uses channel weaves set about six inches apart.

1. Put the dog fifteen feet from pole 1.

2. Stand at pole 5 and face the direction the dog is going.

3. Release the dog. As your dog reaches pole 5, turn in and move briskly backward. You are doing a moving recall past the last pole. Mark the exit and reward as your dog catches you.

With success, backchain one pole at a time through the six poles. This means you stand at pole 4, then pole 3, and so on. For every rep you should start facing forward, and you should move forward with your dog until pole 5. At pole 5 you should continue to turn toward your dog and move briskly backward. Your dog should remain in the poles and should continue to drive toward you as you move backward.

Once your dog is moving with you through the poles, repeat the entire backchain, beginning with pole 5, then pole 4, pole 3, and so on. For this set you remain facing forward past the end of the poles. Thus you are always facing the direction your dog is moving. You should also throw the treat or toy forward as your dog exits past pole 5.

Close the Poles

Your goal is to slowly close the poles and get your dog weaving from a straight entry. This is also where we like to see our students learn to judge how and when to mark entries and exits. Make this a game. Let your dog learn to look for or hunt the poles from a short distance, about fifteen feet for this drill. This phase usually takes several weeks, assuming you are training every day.

This drill uses six poles. Close the weaves in one-inch (channel) or fifteen-degree (weave-a-matic) increments after three or four successful repetitions. Do not cut corners at this stage. Look for 100 percent accuracy. You want your dog successful multiple times before you make the exercise harder.

> Fifteen feet is a good "working distance" for weave poles. On an agility course, your dog should be able to hunt and find the weave poles from fifteen feet.

For the first few reps after each incremental change in the weave spacing, mark the entry and then switch to marking the exit. It is important to reward only a successful completion. As the weaves begin to close, your dog will learn how to move and where to place his feet. His body and foot motions are learned muscle memories. Watch closely for consistent patterns (either hopping or single striding) as you close the weaves. If your dog's style of weaving changes, repeat the previous exercise. It is important that your dog either hop or single stride.

1. Put the dog fifteen feet from pole 1.

2. Move to pole 5 and face the direction the dog is going.

3. Release the dog. Mark the entry/exit. As your dog reaches pole 5, move forward with the dog. As your dog passes the last pole, throw the reward forward. The toy/treat should already be in your hand. Do not get into the habit of reaching for the reward while the dog is weaving. At this training level this leads to anticipation problems, which cause the dog to exit before the last pole.

Trouble Shooting: If your dog skips a pole, remain neutral and try again. If he misses again, open the poles slightly and repeat the drill from the last successful pole.

With success, backchain one pole at a time through the six poles. Your dog should remain in the poles and continue to drive to the end of the poles. Your last two backchain positions are halfway between dog and poles and then even with your dog. Thus each backchain actually has eight steps for the handler. All of the steps should be done before closing the poles incrementally. Remember to switch between marking the entry and marking the exit.

Continue working the weave backchain until the weaves are completely closed. This requires multiple repetitions over many weeks. For example, on channel weaves you should close the weaves in one-inch increments. If you start at six inches, you will eventually do six sets of backchains and work on both the left and right sides.

As you close the weaves, you should also begin to add an obstacle in front of the weave poles. Start with a single, wingless jump. Try using a short, straight tunnel and then try the pause table. Weave poles are a "thinking" exercise. Your dog must concentrate to find the entry and settle into his footwork (hopping or single stride). He must also be able to weave until he runs out of poles and remain focused regardless of when you move. Adding obstacles to the early training can enhance his ability to focus. Do not use the dog walk, A-frame, or seesaw at this level of training.

Expand to Twelve Poles

Once your dog is working six straight poles, it is time to work twelve poles. To ensure success, reopen the weaves poles. Set the channel weaves to about three inches and the weave-a-matics to a forty-five-degree angle. Generally this sets the weaves to the smallest open distance that offers the dog a visible line down the middle. This phase usually takes two weeks, assuming you are training every day.

For this exercise you must mark only the exit. By this point your dog should know the straight-on entry. The goal is to get your dog driving straight on through twelve upright poles.

1. Put the dog fifteen feet from pole 1.

2. Move to pole 6 and face the direction the dog is going.

3. Release the dog. As your dog reaches pole 6, move forward with the dog. Try to stay one pole ahead of the dog.

4. Mark the exit at pole 12 and reward by throwing the toy or treat forward. Keep the reward low to the ground to keep your dog's head down.

Trouble Shooting: If your dog skips a pole, remain neutral and try again. If he misses again, open the poles slightly and repeat the last successful drill.

Through the next couple training sessions, backchain one pole at a time from pole 6 back to pole 1. Your dog should remain in the poles and should continue to drive to the end of the poles. For the last two backchain positions, you should be standing halfway between the dog and the poles and then even with your dog.

Gradually close the weaves one inch or fifteen degrees and continue repeating the backchain. If you start at three inches, you are doing a minimum of three sets of backchains and on both the left and right sides. You may need to close the weaves in half-inch increments after two inches (e.g., three inches, two inches, one and a half inches, one inch, half inch), which means five backchains. It is also important with twelve weaves to walk in a wide loop back to the start and to keep your dog's attention on you. This prevents him from offering the weaves backward (or back weaving).

Your final step with twelve weaves is to do a send into twelve straight poles. Your dog should move ahead of you to find the entry. Try to catch up with the dog around pole 4 or 5 and then move ahead one pole. Reward forward as he exits so your dog learns to exit with drive. Do not proceed forward until your dog is consistently, which means 85 percent or more, driving past pole 12. Anticipation can be a problem with 12 poles. Many dogs weave to pole 10 and then drive forward, skipping the last two poles, often referred to as popping. Making your dog successful at 12 poles during his early training can prevent popping. It is important to work in a quiet area. Do not add distractions. Allow your dog to drive to pole 12 so you can mark it and reward it.

When training weave poles, you must continue to mark the entry intermittently. And if your dog starts missing the entry, isolate the

Dogs can drive through the weaves with a single stride or hop.

behavior—go back a step or two—and mark and reward for several reps. Remember with operant conditioning your dog will offer the behavior that is rewarded. To keep the entries as strong as the exits, you must mark and reward both, though never in the same set. It is also important to mark only one behavior per training session. Be very clear in your mind what you are training—entry? exit? drive? For that session, mark and reward a specific behavior. Do not reward other behaviors, such as the wait before the poles. Rewarding different behaviors waters down or dilutes the conditioning.

If you are working on drive, you can cheer your dog through the poles. If you are working on the entry or exit, then keep the cheering to a minimum. Cheering can easily override the verbal mark for the entry or exit. We also discourage clapping your dog through the weaves. If your dog is dependent on you clapping to either keep his pace up or stay in the poles, you cannot give him a hand signal. Occasional clapping is fine, but do not get your dog habituated to it.

CHAPTER 11

Advanced Weave System

A t Mountain Freaks we do extensive weave-pole training, but there are no gimmicky pieces of equipment or fancy names. It is a foundation and a methodology. We use it for every dog, regardless of size or breed. The idea in weave-entry training is to teach the dog every entry that he may possibly be faced with in his competitive career. We build a rock-solid foundation beginning on day one. It may take a year to get through all the steps in this part of the system, but, if done correctly, the dog will be a great weaver for the duration of his competitive career.

Weaves become a fantastic part of the agility game for most dogs.

Weave Entries

Your dog cannot weave unless he can find the entry. This is a critical skill for every agility dog. One of the more common faults on agility courses, from beginner to master, is the dog not finding the weaves or missing the weave entry. At Mountain Freaks we teach our dogs to hunt for and find the weave entry from twenty-five or thirty feet. And we teach it as an independent behavior. In other words, it is the dog's job. We teach our dogs how to find the weave entry from any location, at any speed, and without micromanagement from the handler.

The intent of the advanced weave training is to teach the dog to find all the angle entries from a moderate pace and then progressively add more complexity and speed. This preserves the foundation entry training and allows the dog to remain successful while building skills needed at the highest level of competition.

The advanced weave system has five levels, each of which has seven stations and five handler actions. The levels represent different configurations of equipment used to increase the degree of difficulty. Level I uses one jump set fifteen feet from the weaves. Level II uses two jumps set fifteen feet apart, with the second jump fifteen feet ahead of the weaves. Level III uses a straight tunnel fifteen feet from the weaves. Level IV uses a jump, a chute, and then the weaves, all spread at fifteen

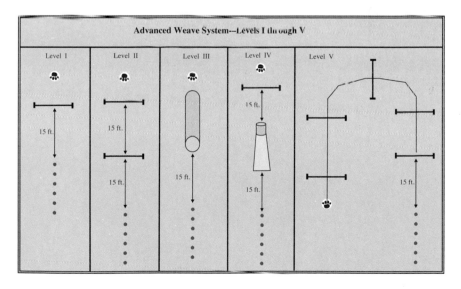

Advanced Weave System--Levels I through V

feet. And Level V uses the weaves in a jump sequence. Every level is worked from all seven stations and with all five handler actions. Thus there are thirty-five (seven stations x five actions) exercises at each level.

All the weave-entry drills have seven stations, or angles, around the first weave pole. The stations are starting points and represent the different angles of approach to the poles. Station 1 is a straight line, or zero-degree entry. Stations 2 and 3 are on thirty-degree angles. Stations 4 and 5 are on sixty-degree angles. And stations 6 and 7 are on ninety-degree angles. The entries from stations 3, 5, and 7 are referred to as "soft-side" entries. From these stations the entry is not visible until the dog goes around the first pole. The entries from stations 2, 4, and 6 are referred to as "hard-side" entries. From these stations the dog can see the entry and approach directly. Initially the hard-side entries are easier for dogs to learn.

At each station there are five handler actions. The actions, which prove your dog's ability to find the weaves independent of your motion, are:

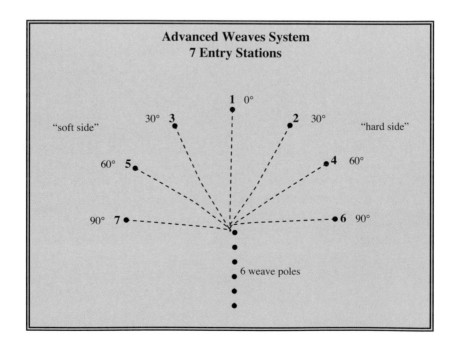

1. dog on left

2. dog on right

3. recall to end of poles

4. rear cross left to right

5. rear cross right to left

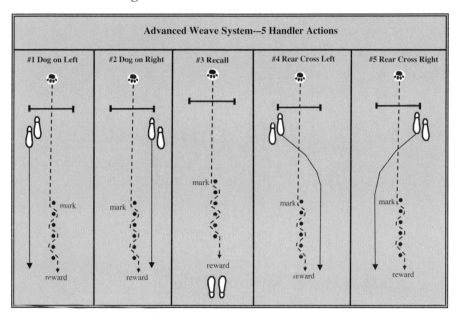

Your goal is to have your dog find the entry regardless of where you are moving. The difficulty increases at each station, with 1 being the easiest and 7 being the hardest. And the complexity increases with each successive handler action. Thus when your dog finds the entry from station 7 (ninety-degree angle) and you are rear crossing from right to left, your dog knows how to enter the weaves!

LEVEL I

The configuration for Level I use a wingless jump set fifteen feet from the poles. All the exercises at all the levels use a full-height jump and only six straight-up poles. Six poles are used for multiple reasons. First, we want the dog and handler focused on the entry. Second, you can do more repetitions without tiring the dog. And third, you have less risk of the dog popping out. What is your response if you mark a correct entry but the dog pops at pole 10? Does he get a reward? For entry training you want to mark the entry and then reward. It is simply easier with six poles to get accurate poles to the exit. We train the dog to stay in all twelve poles with separate exercises and in separate training sessions.

We also do not tell the dog to take the jump. By placing the dog directly in front of the jump, the jump is implied. When you release your dog from the wait, you are sending him to the weaves.

Your advanced weave entry training begins with Level I. Work all seven stations and do all five handler actions at each station before moving on to the next level.

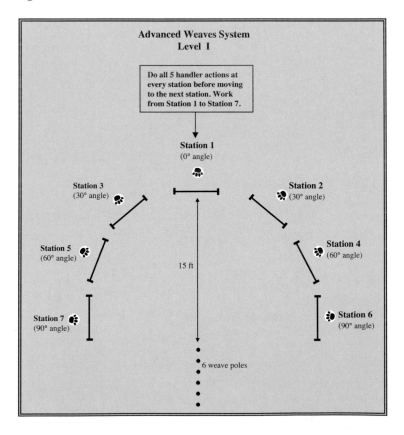

The process is the same for each handler action at each station.

1. Put the dog in a sit a few feet from the jump.

2. Lead out about five feet ahead of the jump, on the same angle as the weave entry. Do not stand on your dog's line to the weaves. You should be slightly to the left or slightly to the right, depending on the action.

3. Release the dog with *Okay. Weave.* Remain stationary. It is your dog's job to find the weave entry as he passes you. Do not help. You can move after your dog passes you, but you should remain several feet behind.

4. Mark the entry with a verbal, such as *Yes!*

5. Catch up to your dog. If possible you should be one pole ahead by pole 6. Regardless, reward with a toy or treat tossed forward and low to the ground. Do not hang back and let the dog wrap the last pole. While working entry drills, it is important not to lose drive. Keep your dog driving forward by rewarding him past the last pole, but do not race him.

With the recalls and at the more difficult angles, it is important to mark the turn to pole 3—not the entry. On a steep angle or in a full stride, your dog may get the entry but may miss the turn from pole 2 to pole 3. It is important to train your eye and wait with the mark to be sure your dog is in the poles and weaving successfully.

When rear crossing do not wait for your dog to make the entry before changing sides. However, on the more difficult angles, you may need to delay your mark until the dog has made the turn from pole 2 to pole 3. If your dog follows your motion (rather than staying in the poles), you may erroneously mark a pullout if you mark his turn to pole 2. It is better not to mark than to mark an incorrect entry.

Training sessions should be limited to five to ten minutes, so you should not be training every station in every session.

Corrections

If your dog misses the entry with any handler action at any station (angle), go neutral. Simply look away for a second and wait. Stay quiet and let your dog absorb the knowledge that something is wrong. Retry from the same station with the same action. If he gets the entry, reward and proceed with exercises. If he misses the entry a third time, you must change the criteria of the drill. For example, at Level I split the distance between the jump and pole 1 but maintain the angle. Hold the dog in a restrained send and release to the poles. If he gets the entry, mark and reward. You can then try the exercise (action and station) again. If he misses a fourth time, you should do a *guided entry*. Walk the dog through the first few poles with a gentle hand in his collar or on a leash for small dogs. Do not mark the entry or reward since you guided the dog and did the work. After guiding the dog through the weaves, backchain through the correction steps to the initial exercise. With success, jackpot and end the session. Your next session should begin at the same level, station, and action at which you ended the previous training session. You should also do more reps at any station/action that have lower success rates.

Accuracy Evaluation

Before advancing to the next station, your dog should be 100 percent successful with all the handler actions. Be patient and consistent with the exercises and the corrections. Do not cut corners. If your dog is persistently missing the entries, go back to the previous station or simplify the exercise. To simplify an exercise you should reduce the distance to pole 1 (thus reducing speed). Your second criterion change should be to reduce the angle, and finally you should open the weaves. Only change one criterion at a time. For example, you should reduce the distance or simplify the angle but not both.

LEVEL II

The configuration for Level II uses two jumps set fifteen feet apart. With the jumps set fifteen feet apart, and another fifteen feet to the weaves, your dog is now over thirty feet away from the poles. You should lead out to the side and midway between the two jumps. Release your dog to the weaves by saying, "Okay. Go weaves!" The execution of the jumps is implied by your releasing the dog to the weaves. Remember to let your dog find the entry ahead of you. Do not race him to the poles and try to influence his line.

Your first correction at this level for a missed entry is to set the dog between jumps 1 and 2. The second correction should be a restrained send from between jumps 1 and 2.

LEVEL III

The next level replaces the two jumps with a straight fifteen-foot tunnel. A tunnel encourages your dog to extend his stride, particularly when you are between the tunnel and the weaves. However, if they approach the weaves in an extended stride, most dogs cannot make the turn from pole 2 to 3. Your dog must learn to collect *before* he gets to the weaves. This is a critical skill for large dogs and for dogs with a high drive. Place your dog at the tunnel entrance and lead out to the end of the tunnel for dog on left, dog on right, rear cross left, and rear cross right. For the recall call your dog through the tunnel and send to the weaves as he exits the tunnel.

LEVEL IV

The next level replaces the tunnel with a chute and a wingless jump. Your dog exits the chute "blind." He cannot see the weaves as he executes the chute, thus finding the weave entry requires concentration and a quick response. Realize your dog is moving forward as he exits the chute, so he must find the entry and adjust his stride accordingly within fifteen feet to hit the entry successfully.

LEVEL V

The final level for advanced weave entries puts the weaves at the end of a five-jump sequence. Place five jumps about fifteen feet apart in a circle or oval and send your dog around to the weaves. You should do both the left and right sides and then both rear crosses. For this level eliminate the recall. The jumps and your motion will encourage your dog to extend his stride. Thus there are only four handler actions at this level.

Twelve-Pole Completion

While you are working entries on six poles, it is also important to work your dog on staying in twelve poles. Entries and twelve-pole completion exercises can be worked simultaneously but never in the same training session. The different exercises balance your dog's ability to find the entry with this ability to weave all the poles—whether there are six, ten, twelve, or sixty—and maintain drive through the entire set. When you are working twelve poles, use an easy, straight-on entry (zero-degree angle) and throw a toy or treat forward as your dog exits. This keeps the focus on the exit (versus the entry), and keeps him driving forward.

Driving through all twelve weave poles is a critical skill.

At Mountain Freaks we use fourteen handler starting positions to proof the dog's ability to stay in the poles. For these exercises you should mark only the exit. And the exit is different depending on where the dog is going after the poles. If the dog is going straight or turning right, he must wrap around pole 12. If the dog is turning left after the poles, he only has to weave eleven poles. He does not have to pass pole 12 before turning. For this reason we work two different exits from the poles. If the handler is to the right of the poles with the dog on the left, we mark after the dog turns his head around pole 12. Conversely, if the handler is to the left of the poles with the dog on the right, we mark as the dog's head passes between poles 11 and 12.

For all of these exercises, we make the entry easy (straight on or zero-degree angle). There is also no obstacle before the weaves. The dog should be about fifteen feet away from the poles, and you should lead

Keep your dog driving forward through the poles.

out about five feet in front of the dog. The starting positions, which proof your dog's ability to stay in the weaves independent of your motion, are:

1. dog on left

2. dog on right

3. recall to end of twelve poles

4. ten-foot lateral distance (dog on left)

5. ten-foot lateral distance (dog on right)

6. send through poles (handler stays back)

7. twenty-foot lateral distance (dog on left)

8. twenty-foot lateral distance (dog on right)

9. pull off to the left (ten to twelve feet)

10. pull off to the right (ten to twelve feet)

11. pull off to the left to the landing side of a jump set perpendicular to the end of the weave poles (reward dog on landing side of jump)

12. pull off to the left to a tunnel perpendicular to the weave poles (handler pulls off to end of tunnel)

13. pull off to the right to a tunnel perpendicular to the weave poles (handler pulls off to end of tunnel)

For all of these exercises, mark the exit point—between poles 11 and 12 or after pole 12—with a verbal such as *Yes!* and follow the dog down the poles. Reward with a toy or treat tossed forward. Do not hang back and let the dog wrap the last pole. Keep your dog driving forward by rewarding him past the last pole, but do not race him.

When you are at a lateral distance or pulling off (moving laterally away) from your dog while he is weaving, support him in the poles with an extended arm (similar to the out drill). You should also put out a cone or other marker for steps 4, 5, 7, and 8 to keep your line straight. Do not veer in (or out) when moving at a lateral distance. For all the pull-off exercises, you should be moving with your dog through pole 7 and then curving away. As you begin to move away, extend your arm to keep your dog in the poles.

If the dog pulls out of the poles, stop and be neutral. Do not praise or reward. Go back and try the exercise again. If the dog misses for a second time, then change the criterion. You should go back to the prior handler starting point. For the entry drills there are four steps to the correction process. For twelve-pole completion drills, there are only two. Make it easier sooner and get a high rate of success before changing the criteria.

As your training progresses, there are all sorts of proofing exercises that you can do. You can throw a toy or treat through the poles while the dog is weaving, have a training partner walk through the poles ahead or behind the dog, or have another dog weave a second set of poles in the opposite direction. In all of these proofs, you mark as soon as the dog passes the distraction, assuming he is still weaving of course.

Weave Theory

In summary, the basic tenants beneath the Mountain Freaks advanced weave system include the following:

- Weave proficiency is 100 percent and 0 percent handling. Most weave errors are due to incomplete training, not handling errors. Common mistakes in training include the following:

  - improper marking (either timing or marking a dog that does not understand marking)

- no marking

- over-rewarding a sub-par behavior or rewarding in the wrong position

- Weaving is an independent obstacle. Unlike jumping and sequencing, your dog should learn to weave regardless of your position and motion. This includes both entries and twelve-pole completion.

- Dogs should be able to "hunt" for the weaves and adjust their own line—at any speed—to make the entry and stay in the poles through the first two turns.

- Dogs should decelerate (rock back) as necessary to make the entry and then accelerate through the remaining poles.

- Weaves are a "thinking" exercise and should be done first in training sessions.

- At this level, entries and twelve-pole completion must be trained in different sessions.

- When training, short sessions done several times a day work best. Always start with a hungry, well-rested dog. The number of sessions is dependent on the dog's natural drive and interest in the poles. Always quit training when your dog is still in drive and has just earned a jackpot.

CHAPTER 12

Types of Agility Events

A s a competitive sport agility offers a multitude of competition levels, games, and events. There are a dozen different organizations sanctioning agility events in the United States, and every organization has different rules and classes. Depending on your abilities, interests, and time commitment, you may find one organization better suited to your needs than another. Review and evaluate the different organizations with your instructor or experienced agility competitors. The following organizations sponsor agility competitions—either trials (titling or qualifying events) or matches (practice or for-fun events). Each has specific rules for equipment choices, obstacle performance, and titles.

American Kennel Club

The AKC offers three types of agility classes for purebred dogs registered with the club or who have an ILP number, which allows a nonregistered purebred dog to compete in performance events. The Standard class includes jumps, tunnels, weave poles, and the contact obstacles, such as the dog walk, A-frame, pause table, and seesaw. The second class is Jumpers with Weaves, which has jumps, tunnels, and weave poles. The third and newest class is the Fifteen and Send Time (FAST) class. Given a set course time, handlers select obstacles and sequences to accumulate points prior to completing a short course (three to five obstacles) designated by the judge that must be handled at a distance. The FAST class is considered a strategy game.

Dogs are eligible to compete in agility events once they are fifteen months old. All the AKC classes are offered at increasing levels of difficulty, from novice to masters, but all dogs begin at the novice level. In order to make the competition equal between the different sizes of dogs, classes are divided into jump heights (eight-inch, twelve-inch, sixteen-inch, twenty-inch, twenty-four-inch, and twenty-six-inch), with different course times for each height division. The AKC also offers Preferred classes, which have lower jump heights and time bonuses. Titles are earned at the Novice, Open, Excellent, and Masters levels. A title is awarded to the dog who earns the three qualifying scores in a class.

After obtaining an Excellent Standard and Excellent Jumpers title, a dog and handler team can earn a Master Agility Champion (MACH) title. This elite title has two requirements. The dog must qualify (get a Q) in both the Excellent Standard and Excellent Jumpers classes at a trial, thus earning a double Q. Twenty double Qs are required to earn a MACH *and* the dog must accumulate 750 speed points. Speed points are earned by deducting the dog's time on the course from the judge's set course time.

In addition to trials in all fifty states, the AKC sponsors matches, which are practice trials, and two national-level competitions. The Agility Invitational invites the top five dogs—based on MACH point accumulations for the year—of each recognized breed to compete in a round-robin competition. This event showcases the best of each breed. A second event, the Agility Nationals, draws the top competitors in every height division to compete head-on in an exciting two-day event. At the end of two days, the top ten to fifteen competitors compete for a National Championship. The AKC also sponsors three teams that compete annually at the FCI World Cup Invitational Agility Trial, which is held in Europe.

For more information on the AKC and its agility program, go to www.akc.org.

Australian Shepherd Club of America

In 1995 the Australian Shepherd Club of America (ASCA) incorporated agility into its competitive programs. ASCA agility trials are open to *any* dog—purebred or mixed breed—that is at least eighteen months old. There are three levels of competition—Novice, Open, and Elite—and there are three titling classes—Regular, Jumpers, and Gamblers. Within the program there are three divisions: standard, veterans (dogs seven years and older or a handler who is sixty years and older or a disabled handler), and junior handlers (open to handlers who are seventeen years old or younger). ASCA recognizes four height divisions: eight-inch, twelve-inch, sixteen-inch, and twenty-inch, with twenty-four-inch being optional. They also allow a dozen different breeds, such as Welsh Corgi, Bassett hounds, and Staffordshire bull terriers, to jump lower heights.

Title certificates are awarded once a dog has attained thirty points in a regular class, which has contact obstacles, jumps, tunnels, and weave poles; twenty points in a jumpers class, which has only jumps and tunnels; and twenty points for a gambler class, which has obstacles, jumps, weaves, and tunnels. The gamblers class has two parts. The handler course (or point-accumulation segment) is run for points and is followed by the gamble (or independent segment), in which the handler must stay a certain distance, as defined by the judge, away from the dog. Dogs earn an ATCH—Agility Trial Championship—by earning points in the Elite division. The ASCA Agility Nationals are held annually at the ASCA National Specialty.

For more information on ASCA and its agility program, go to www .asca.org.

Canine Performance Events

Growing in popularity in both America and Canada, Canine Performance Events (CPE) offer titling classes in agility for purebred and mixed-breed dogs that are fifteen months of age or older. Using the dog's height at the shoulder, CPE categorizes dogs into one of six jump heights, which are four-inch, eight-inch, twelve-inch, sixteen-inch, twenty-inch, and twenty-four-inch. There are multiple levels of competition: 1, 2, 3, 4, 5, and C. Level 1 is for beginner dogs and/or beginner handlers, and Level C is for experienced dog-and-handler teams working toward an Agility Trial Championship. CPE allows dogs to begin competing at Level 1, 2, or 3. Within each level, CPE offers multiple layers of competition including regular, veterans/enthusiast (for dogs that jump four-inches below their regular height or that are six years or older), and specialist (for dogs that jump eight-inches below their regular height).

With an emphasis on fun, CPE offers more than half a dozen different classes and four title categories at every level. The Standard class contains jumps, weaves, tunnels, and contact obstacles. The Colors class offers two overlapping, mini-agility courses on the same field and challenges the team to navigate one course successfully in the allotted time. The Wildcard class, using all the obstacles from the Standard class, offers multiple wild card options that the team must choose to collect points. Snooker is a strategy game that challenges the planning ability of the handler, who must select obstacles and sequences to earn points, and the focus of the dog, who must follow the handler's directions. Another strategy game, Jackpot, requires considerable course planning and distance handling. This class is run in two pieces: point accumulation and a gamble. The Jumpers class contains single jumps, spread jumps, and tunnels. And finally, CPE offers a Fullhouse class, which challenges the team to execute a pair of obstacles, three of a kind, and a joker (or wild card obstacle) in the short time allowed.

There are four title categories recognized by CPE. A Standard title is earned with qualifying runs in a Standard class. A Handler title is earned with qualifying runs in Colors and Wildcard. A Strategy title is earned with qualifying runs in Jackpot and Snooker. And a Fun title is earned with qualifying runs in Jumpers and Fullhouse. The number of qualifying runs varies for each level. In addition, dogs can earn an Agility Trial Championship and an Agility Team Extraordinaire title by collecting points from Level C classes.

For more information on CPE, go to www.k9cpe.com.

Dogs on Course North America

Established in 2005, Dogs on Course North America (DOCNA) is one of the newest dog agility venues. With a focus on fun and flow, DOCNA offers agility for all levels of dogs and handlers, from the very competitive to the more casual weekend warrior, and to the dog that is getting older to the junior handler. Competitors choose the classes and division or level that allow them to challenge their abilities and develop their skills at their own pace and meet their own goals. Both mixed-breed and purebred dogs are eligible for registration with DOCNA. Dogs can compete at twelve months or older in the first two levels, but they must be fifteen months old to compete at the highest level.

DOCNA offers three levels: Beginner, Intern, and Specialist. Any team can begin with Beginner and work through Intern into Specialist, although teams with titles in other registries can grandfather into the level of their choice. Within each level there are multiple divisions: competition, select (lower jump heights and extra time allocated), veterans (dogs over seven years of age or handler over sixty years of age), grand vet (dog over ten years of age or handler over sixty with dog over seven years of age), and junior handler.

With jump heights ranging from four inches to twenty-four inches, DOCNA has six classes. The first class is Standard, which has weaves, jumps, tunnels, and contact obstacles. The strategy classes are Traditional Gamblers and Strategic Time Gamblers. And fun classes include Jumpers, Snakes 'n Ladders, and Trigility, which is a team event. Championship events are offered by area (eastern and western).

For more information about DOCNA, go to www.docna.com.

4-H Dog Agility

Geared toward the beginner junior handler, 4-H agility was founded in the early 1990s. The 4-H program emphasizes safety, control, and fun. In order to begin taking 4-H agility classes, a dog/handler team must have achieved a minimum obedience score of 180 or higher at a county, regional, or state 4-H dog show or must have completed two years of obedience training. Dogs must be a minimum of twelve months old, and it is recommended that larger breeds be at least eighteen months old.

Jump heights are six inches, twelve inches, and eighteen inches. There are five levels of competition: Beginner, Elementary, Intermediate, Senior, and Advanced. At the Beginner level, the course is a simple

S, M, or U shape with a low A-frame, pause table, pipe tunnel, chute, and six jumps. The allowed time is sixty seconds, and the dog is kept on leash. The requirements at the Elementary level are the same, except the dog is run off leash. The Intermediate level requires a course design that is slightly more challenging than a figure eight and has more obstacles, including the dog walk and six weave poles. At the Senior level the course is more challenging (equivalent to an AKC Novice or USDAA Starters/Beginner course) and has thirteen to sixteen obstacles. The Advanced level has more obstacles and more course challenges, including twelve weaves and higher contacts.

In addition to allowing members to begin competing with dogs that are still in training, the 4-H program has several other advantages for junior handlers. The pause table is always a down. Most faults are charged a five-point penalty (versus being an eliminating or failing fault in other registries) And all 4-H agility shows are allowed a familiarization. In Beginner and Elementary classes, this consists of walking the dog over each contact obstacle, tunnel, pause table, and a maximum of two jumps. In the Intermediate and Senior classes, it consists of all contact obstacles, tire, and weave poles. Other obstacles may be included at the judge's discretion. Each competitor may have up to three attempts at each obstacle, but any given obstacle may be completed only one time. There are also more placements allowed per class.

Not all state and county 4-H organizations offer dog agility. For more information go to www.4husa.org and open the link to your state's 4-H program.

North American Dog Agility Council

The North American Dog Agility Council (NADAC) was founded by Sharon Nelson in St. Maries, Idaho. It was formed in 1993 to provide dogs and handlers with a fast, safe, and enjoyable form of the sport of dog agility. The purpose of a NADAC agility trial is to demonstrate the ability of a dog and his handler to work as a smoothly functioning team. All dogs must be registered with NADAC to compete in their sanctioned events, which are hosted by affiliated agility clubs. Registration is a one-time process, and the number assigned is permanent. Any healthy dog, purebred or mixed breed, over eighteen months of age is eligible to compete in NADAC trials.

With separate class divisions for veterans and junior handlers and a variety of games, NADAC offers something for everyone. The Junior Handler division is open to any dog whose handler is seventeen years of age or younger. The host group may choose to divide the junior handler classes into two different groups, youths age eleven and under and youths twelve and over. The Veterans division is open to any dog age seven or older or a dog whose handler is age sixty or older. This division is also open to any handler who has a certificate of disability, regardless of the age of the dog.

Within the Junior Handler and Veteran divisions, a dog may jump a maximum of sixteen inches. In the other divisions heights range from four inches to twenty inches, with over two dozen breeds given jump-height exceptions, which allow them to jump at a lower height. Each division has three levels: Novice, Open, and Elite. And, every class in a NADAC trial is split into two categories: Proficient and Skilled. Courses and times are the same for both categories. In the Proficient category, dogs must jump their measured jump height. Runs must be clean, with no course faults or time faults, in order to qualify. In the Skilled category all runs must be clean to qualify, except in Regular, where dogs may still earn five-point qualifiers for any run with five or fewer faults. The Skilled category also allows the dog to jump one height lower than they are required to jump in the Proficient category.

Classes are Regular, Chances, Jumpers, Tunnelers, Touch 'n Go, and Weavers. The Regular class tests the dog's ability to perform all the obstacles safely with the pace increasing at each level. The goal of the Jumpers class is to demonstrate the ability of the handler and dog to work as a fast-moving, smooth functioning team over jumps. The goal of the Tunnelers class is to demonstrate the dog's ability to respond quickly to directional commands from the handler while negotiating a course comprised of only tunnels. The Weavers class showcases the dog's ability to correctly enter weave poles at a variety of angles and weave accurately at speed on a course comprised of tunnels and weave poles. Touch 'n Go demonstrates the dog's ability to perform contact obstacles correctly on a course comprised of tunnels and four to five contact obstacles. The goal of the Chances class is to test the distance, directional, and discrimination skills of the dog and handler team over a sequence of ten to fifteen obstacles.

For each class, in both the Proficient and Skilled categories, NADAC offers certificates that acknowledge the achievement of the basic title in that class/level, as well as titles that show advanced performance. Each title has specific points requirements. In addition to the titles, NADAC offers special awards and certificates that acknowledge higher levels of performance across multiple classes and levels, including a NATCH–NADAC Agility Trial Champion.

For additional information about NADAC, go to www.nadac.com.

Teacup Dog Agility Association

The purpose of the Teacup Dog Agility Association is to provide a competitive venue for dogs of small stature, regardless of breed or pedigree. Teacup Agility encourages smaller courses with tighter transitional distances between obstacles. In Teacup action the average distance between obstacles is set at six to eight feet, so the marathon loping between obstacles that small dogs have to endure on other agility courses does not occur. The small dog encounters obstacles at a pace proportional to his size. Of course this means the Teacup handler has to be smart in his timing and keen on his feet. Additionally, obstacles such as tunnels, the seesaw, the A-frame, and the dog walk are scaled down to size for small dogs.

The date of the first Teacup trial was May 19, 2002, in Kansas City, Kansas. Thirty-two dogs were entered. Three other trials were quickly followed in Columbus, Ohio; Manchester, New Hampshire; and Eugene, Oregon. Today there are over 1,900 dogs registered in Teacup Agility, representing eighty-one breeds, including All American, and spreading across thirty-nine states, Mexico, and Canada. Teacup has sanctioned agility clubs in eighteen states.

Teacup Agility is open to all dogs who measure seventeen inches or less at the shoulder and are at least twelve months of age. Jump heights range from four inches to sixteen inches, with adjustments for long-backed and short-legged dogs. There is no restriction on account of breed or pedigree. There are three levels: Beginner, Intermediate, and Superior. Every trial offers two Standard classes and many offer a variety of games classes. The Standard class requires dogs to traverse twelve to twenty obstacles, depending on the dog's competition level.

Dogs can also be fast-tracked in Teacup Agility. If you have an advanced title with another club, you may choose to enter the corresponding Teacup level. You do not need to begin in Beginners. Dogs must be registered with Teacup Agility to run at a sanctioned trial. Titles are offered at all levels, including Superior and Q, and for all classes. A Teacup Agility Championship (TACH) can also be earned.

For more information about Teacup Agility, go to www.k9tdaa .com.

United States Dog Agility Association

Organized in 1986 to introduce the sport of dog agility to North America, USDAA adopted the motto "Promoting International Standards for Dog Agility." USDAA is one of the largest and oldest agility organizations in the United States. Initially the agility program was patterned after the British standards, but the USDAA quickly evolved into an international organization with a diverse certification and competition program. With more than twenty-two thousand registered competitors and more than thirty thousand dogs representing more than two hundred different breeds of dogs, including mix breeds, the USDAA represents more than a hundred affiliated groups who conduct more than five hundred events each year throughout the continental United States, Puerto Rico, Canada, Mexico, Bermuda, Guatemala, Costa Rica, and Japan.

Dogs must be registered with the USDAA in order to compete in sanctioned events and are eligible to compete upon reaching eighteen months of age. The USDAA recognizes four basic height divisions within each of its competitive programs. The Championship program, where dogs jump twelve inches, sixteen inches, twenty-two inches, or twenty-six inches, was developed to be congruous with international standards. The Performance program was developed for recreational competition purposes, with slightly lower jump heights set at eight inches, twelve inches, sixteen inches, and twenty-two inches. The Performance program also offers generous time constraints and a lower A-frame for all height classes.

USDAA participants earn certification titles at three levels: Started, Advanced, and Masters. Certification titles are offered for both Standard and Nonstandard classes. The Standard class is the foundation class in the sport of dog agility. All obstacles are utilized, including three contact obstacles, an A-frame, dog walk, and seesaw, two types of tunnels, weave poles, table, tire jump, and a variety of hurdles and jumps, all of which are set in a sequence designed by the judge. The Nonstandard classes are Gambler's Choice, Snooker, Jumpers, and Pairs. Gamblers is a point-basis class wherein handlers develop their own strategy for running a course in order to accumulate as many points as possible during the time allotted by the judge. Snooker, named after the billiards game popular in Great Britain, is another point-basis class. Teams collect points by completing obstacles in "snooker" sequence, which is defined by color. A red obstacle is followed by a color obstacle, which is given a point value. However, the team must successfully perform the red obstacle to earn the right to perform the color obstacle and earn the points. Jumpers excludes all contact obstacles. It is principally comprised of hurdles and tunnels, although it may also include weave poles. Pairs classes are those that include two or more dog-and-handler teams competing on a course together. The course may be split, wherein each team member runs a segment, or each team member may run the entire course. A course may include all the obstacles other than the table, which can only be used as a start, finish, or baton-exchange point.

USDAA provides recognition for a wide variety of accomplishments. Titles are offered for all programs, levels, and classes. For those who excel, competitors may earn the coveted Agility Dog Champion. In addition the USDAA hosts three international tournament series: the Grand Prix of Dog Agility World Championships, the $10,000 Dog Agility Steeplechase, and the Dog Agility Masters Three-Dog Team Championship. Each has enjoyed national television coverage in recent years, with the Grand Prix being the longest-running tournament series in the western hemisphere and one of the most prestigious tournaments in the sport today.

The USDAA organization also sponsors teams who compete in several prestigious tournaments each year in Europe.

For more information about USDAA, go to www.usdaa.com.

United Kennel Club

Established in 1898, the UKC is the largest all-breed, performance-dog registry in the world, registering dogs from all fifty states and twenty-five foreign countries. Although more than 60 percent of its twelve thousand annually licensed events are tests of hunting ability and instinct, the UKC also sponsors conformation, obedience, and agility events. The organization prides itself on its family-oriented, friendly, educational events and supports a *total dog* philosophy. Its events are designed for dogs that look and perform equally well. In addition to their purebred dog registry, UKC offers a Limited Privilege program, which is open to all dogs, regardless of pedigree, that are spayed or neutered.

The UKC agility program offers three jump heights: eight inches, fourteen inches, and twenty inches. Courses consist of thirteen to sixteen obstacles from three obstacle categories: hurdle, nonhurdle, and pause. Compared to other agility organizations, the UKC venue has a wider variety of equipment, including a crawl tunnel, window and log jumps, a water hurdle, a picket fence hurdle, a sway bridge, and a swing plank. There are two levels: United Agility I (UAGI) and United Agility II (UAGII). Upon completion of the UAGI and UAGII titles, dog and handler teams can begin working on a United Agility Champion (UACH) title. Every year the top fifty dogs in each level are invited to participate in an Agility All-Star Invitational competition.

For more information about the UKC, go to www.ukcdogs.com.

Today dozens of local agility trials, tournaments, and challenge events are held every weekend across the United States. Tournaments have expanded into weeklong events that showcase the incredible talents of every type of dog. National media coverage of events, like the

AKC Agility Invitational, USDAA Tournament of Champions, Purina's Incredible Dog Challenge, and the Clean Run 60 Weave Pole Challenge, has drawn more interest and attention to the sport every year.

Each organization and competition has a particular set of rules, but the equipment and course flows are similar. Different venues offer different types of competition and offer enough variety so that everyone with an agility dog can have fun. Whether you enter a fun match twice a year or compete every weekend and holiday, agility can and will provide unique challenges. Every agility course is different and each level of competition tests the handler's skills, the dog's training, and their ability to work as a team. The bottom line: Agility training can take you and your dog wherever you decide to go.

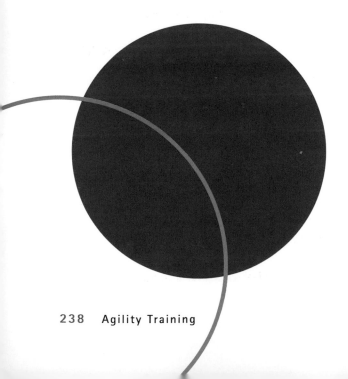

Index

About the Authors

Ali Canova

Competing in dog sports since 1993, Ali Canova has trained a wide variety of breeds including English springer spaniels, papillions, golden retrievers, and Border collies. With her Border collies, Ali has become one of America's top agility competitors.

Besides competing at a national level, Ali is codirector of Mountain Freaks Agility, where she has developed and perfected an agility training system that emphasizes teamwork and foundation training. She provides private and class instruction for some of the top agility competitors across the country and is also in demand as an instructor at agility camps and for seminars across the country.

Dr. Joe Canova

Owner and codirector of Mountain Freaks Agility, Joe Canova has been involved in the sport of dog agility since 1996 and is a national-level competitor. Joe has had multiple dogs in the national finals of both the AKC and USDAA championships and has qualified for and competed at the AKC World Team Tryouts for the past three years with his Border collie, Argos, who is an AKC and USDAA agility champion. Joe is also an instructor at Mountain Freaks and provides seminars with his wife, Ali Canova.

Diane Goodspeed

After retiring as a business analyst in 2001, Diane Goodspeed became an author and an agility competitor and instructor. With an eclectic mix of breeds, including a Border collie, a Shetland sheepdog, and Lhasa apsos, Diane has competed since 1992 in obedience, herding, and agility. She has qualified a dog for every AKC Agility Championship since 2000. In 2006 her sheltie, trained under Ali Canova, qualified for and attended the AKC Agility Nationals in January, completed his AKC agility championship in June, and won the All-Star Performance

Dog tournament in August. In addition to teaching agility classes and private clients, Diane has published two books in the past two years.

For more information on Mountain Freaks, please go to www .mountainfreaksagility.com. Joe and Ali also have training DVDs available. In 2007 Joe produced *World Class Weaves!* This DVD showcases Joe's weave-pole method and is an excellent companion to this book. Ali's *Running Contact* DVD explains her extensive training methods for developing running contacts on the A-frame and dog walk. Both can be ordered from Clean Run Productions (www.cleanrun.com) or direct from Mountain Freaks.

Catcher is airborne over the A-frame. (Photo courtesy of Joe Canova)